Selected Poems

Selected Poems
Al Purdy

McClelland and Stewart Limited
Toronto/Montreal

©1972 by Al Purdy

PAPER 0-7710-7196-5
CASE 0-7710-7198-1

The Canadian Publishers
McClelland and Stewart Limited
25 Hollinger Road, Toronto 374

Note:
Some of these poems are slightly
revised, others not. The Canada
Council must also take some
responsibility: a number of
them would not have been written
but for funds provided by the
Council.

A.W.P.

Introduction by George Woodcock/8

THE ROAD TO NEWFOUNDLAND/17
OVER THE HILLS IN THE RAIN, MY DEAR/19
THE RUNNERS/21
THE CARIBOO HORSES/24
LATE RISING AT ROBLIN LAKE/25
THE DRUNK TANK/26
MY GRANDFATHER TALKING—30 YEARS AGO/28
OLD ALEX/29
SPRING SONG/30
ONE RURAL WINTER/32
WINTER AT ROBLIN LAKE/34
ROBLIN'S MILLS (1)/34
DARK LANDSCAPE/36
INTERRUPTION/38
IDIOT'S SONG/39
MY GRANDFATHER'S COUNTRY/40
MARRIED MAN'S SONG/42
PERCY LAWSON/44
NOTES ON A FICTIONAL CHARACTER/46
HOME-MADE BEER/48
DYLAN/49
FIDEL CASTRO IN REVOLUTIONARY SQUARE/50
HOMBRE/52
DREAM OF HAVANA/54
SERGEANT JACKSON/56
ABOUT BEING A MEMBER OF OUR ARMED FORCES/58
ARCTIC RHODODENDRONS/59
THE TURNING POINT/60
TREES AT THE ARCTIC CIRCLE/62
WASHDAY/64
THE SCULPTORS/67
WHEN I SAT DOWN TO PLAY THE PIANO/69

LAMENT FOR THE DORSETS/71
AT THE MOVIES/73
WHAT DO THE BIRDS THINK?/75
THE COUNTRY OF THE YOUNG/77
HELPING MY WIFE GET SUPPER/79
HOUSE GUEST/80
COLLECTING THE SQUARE ROOT OF MINUS ONE/82
AT ROBLIN LAKE/84
POEM/86
WILDERNESS GOTHIC/87
POEM FOR ONE OF THE ANNETTES/88
LOVE SONG/90
NECROPSY OF LOVE/91
THE WINEMAKER'S BEAT-ÉTUDE/92
NEWS REPORTS AT AMELIASBURG/94
DEATH OF JOHN F. KENNEDY/96
ON THE DECIPHERMENT OF "LINEAR B"/99
HOCKEY PLAYERS/100
JOINT ACCOUNT/103
EVERGREEN CEMETERY/104
AT THE QUINTE HOTEL/106
WATCHING TRAINS/108
COMPLAINT LODGED WITH THE L.C.B.O./110
FROM THE CHIN P'ING MEI/111
BOUNDARIES/112
WHOEVER YOU ARE/113
FURTHER DEPONENT SAITH NOT/114
ROBLIN'S MILLS (2)/116
THE COUNTRY NORTH OF BELLEVILLE/118
MY '48 PONTIAC/120
TRANSIENT/122

Index of titles/124
Index of first lines/126

On the Poetry of Al Purdy.

Al Purdy's writing fits Canada like a glove; you can feel the fingers of the land working through his poems. I suppose that is why, the deeper I have gone in understanding the country and the more I have found myself a surprised patriot, the closer I have felt to Purdy as man and poet.

But this is not the reason why I first became interested in him. Writers who are contemporaries often come together in the beginning for odd, inconsequential reasons. Twelve years ago – or perhaps only eleven – I wrote a play, *Maskerman,* which the CBC produced, and out of the northern wilds of British Columbia, up near Hazelton, came a postcard in an unknown hand complimenting me on a fine *decadent* piece of work, which was precisely the effect I had been seeking. I was further disposed towards Purdy when I learnt that he had spent the war at the only place on earth that bears my name – the minute whistlestop hamlet of Woodcock somewhere in the lost lands between Prince George and Prince Rupert.

This was enough to set me reading Purdy, still, in the early Sixties, awaiting his sudden and splendid arrival as a major contemporary poet. I met him shortly afterwards, and realized that we shared a total absence of any original connection with academe and all it meant. We were both autodidacts, omnivorous readers, furious generalists, restless travellers, maverick radicals, gluttons for variety of experience, interested in the assemblage of every kind of apparent irrelevancy. We were amateur historians, backyard philosophers, jacks-of-many-trades who had built houses with our own hands and learnt what we knew by our own efforts. Rare types a decade ago when every other poet in the groves except Milton Acorn seemed to sport at least an M.A., for those were the days before the Great Dropout began.

The matter at hand is Purdy's poetry, not his persona, but I think what I have said is relevant because it illustrates two facts that are necessary to an appreciation of Purdy as poet; that he *is* the kind of poet with whom one's first contact can be a postcard sent from among the totem poles in decayed Indian villages far to the north, and that he is also a man of vast and miscellaneous knowledge which constantly flows in and out of the open ends of his poetry.

I began by talking of the glovelike closeness of Purdy's poetry to Canada as one experiences the country, and there is no doubt of his deep intuitive grasp of the nature of the land, of the character of its history, though to claim him as purely a Canadian poet would be to do him an immense injustice. But Canada – and Loyalist Ontario in particular – is indeed the heart of his world, of which he can say:

and if I must commit myself to love
for any one thing
it will be here in the red glow
where failed farms sink back into earth
the clearings join and fences no longer divide
where the running animals gather their bodies together
and pour themselves upward
into the tips of falling leaves
with mindless faith that presumes a future

Out of that land where the wilderness seeps back over the labours of a past generation, Purdy's poetic eye journeys eastward to Newfoundland, with its lost memories of the Vikings (curiously skipping Quebec as he also skips the Prairies), westward to British Columbia, which he knew in the Thirties long before it became a special haven of poets, northward to the Arctic. These extremities of the land are the poles between which he suspends his vision of Canada, a vision that interprets geography and history as interpenetrating versions of each other. To further narrow his vision, it is essentially a rural one, which hardly recognizes a city except Vancouver (deurbanized by the penetrating sea), and it is based on the knowledge, which most Canadians are curiously anxious to avoid, that this is, even in human terms, an ancient and not a new land, a land already beginning to decay into maturity.

The very spinning point of his world, its watery omphalos which in Canadian eyes may some day become the equivalent of Walden Pond, is Roblin Lake near the lost Loyalist hamlet of Ameliasburgh ("named after a German dumpling named Amelia"), where Purdy built his house among the larruping frogs and above the silent pike, and about which so many of his poems are written. Perhaps one can take these Roblin Lake poems, like Roblin Lake itself, as master fragments in the mosaic of Purdy's vision. What they are about is place and change and continuity. Some of them are elegies for those who built the stone mills of Old Upper Canada, most of them now more vanished than the Breton megaliths:

The black millpond
            holds them
movings and reachings and fragments
the gear and tackle of living
under the water eye
all things laid aside
                  discarded
                        forgotten
but they had their being once
and left a place to stand on

Yet it is not ghosts only that appear in Purdy's eye, nor merely old men like his grandfather talking long ago of a day when there was

nothin but moonlight boy
nothin but woods...

For what makes him a real rural poet, as distinct from a country sentimentalist, is his concreteness of view, an awareness of the brilliant surface of the earth as clear as that of an imagist, and yet at the same time a sense of depths and heights, of superreal dimensions, so that common things can suddenly become irradiated and the world swing into ecstasy.

But not too much into ecstasy for the existential relations to continue, and the vision of place to be poised between tradition and change, as in "Wilderness Gothic", one of his most completely successful poems, where he is watching a man across Roblin Lake repairing a church spire, working his way up towards its vanishing point, as if his faith pushed him beyond it. It is one of the poems in which Purdy deftly juxtaposes the different elements of his world, for as the man works at patching the edifice of a dying religion, the life of nature goes on in its old merciless way.

Fields around are yellowing into harvest,
nestling and fingerling are sky and water borne,
death is yodelling quiet in green woodlots,
and bodies of three young birds have disappeared
in the sub-surface of the new county highway...

But the picture, as Purdy says, "is incomplete" without the "gothic ancestors" the church suggests, and with the thought of them and their disappearance, together with many generations since, an ominous tone vibrates in the whole scene.

An age and a faith moving into transition,
the dinner cold and new-baked bread a failure,
deep woods shiver and water drops hang pendant,
double yolked eggs and the house creaks a little—
Something is about to happen. Leaves are still.
Two shores away, a man hammering in the sky.
Perhaps he will fall.

It is indeed a shadowed world that Purdy often presents, a world in which

We have set traps
and must always remember
to avoid them ourselves.

We forget our forebears and yet in ways we do not recognize we share their predicament. In the first poem of this collection, "The Road to Newfoundland", Purdy applies to driving a car what at first seems a far-fetched metaphor:

My foot has pushed a fire ahead of me
for a thousand miles...

But as the poem continues we realize that he is reading time depth by depth to the primal human dependence on fire:

A long time's way here since stone

age man carried the fire-germ
in a moss-lined basket
from camp to camp
and prayed to it...

And when he comes to talk later in the poem of his flesh "captive to a steel extension of myself", we realize he is saying that it is the general condition of man, who owes his civilization to his tools, to be enslaved by his technology. But the situation is reciprocal; the technology is captive too, and this is a paradox without end as Purdy suggests when, at poem's close, he imagines himself driving

steadily north
with the captive fire
in cool evening
towards the next camp

North, like West, is a cardinal direction for Purdy (as South over the border most certainly is not), and it is in some of his Arctic poems that he becomes most purely the poet of place, though even here it is often still the kind of dialogue between the man and his environment with its finned and feathered and flowered inhabitants, which is almost incessant at Roblin Lake, going on in other ways. In "Trees in the Arctic Circle" he sets off in a kind of parody of Lawrence's *Birds, Beasts and Flowers*, reproaching the dwarf willows for their cowardice in crawling under rocks and grovelling among lichens; trees should be proud like Douglas firs or "oaks like gods in autumn gold". And yet, he tells himself, they are going about their business of making sure in the only way they can that the species does not die out, and he brings himself to a statement that might be taken as a summary of his sense of the brotherhood of life:

To take away the dignity
            of any living thing
even tho it cannot understand
            the scornful words
is to make life itself trivial...

And the next poem is in fact a pure lyrical celebration of the beauty of the rapid springtime florescence of the North, "Arctic Rhododendrons."

Yet even from the Arctic the best poem Purdy brought back was that grave and beautiful meditation on the fate of man and the nature of art, "Lament for the Dorsets", those massive early Eskimos who appear to have been made extinct five or six hundred years ago by the competition of smaller men whose dog-drawn sleighs were more effective than those the Dorsets dragged by hand. He wonders if the Dorsets really knew what was happening to them, and behind that thought whispers the hint that modern man, so different from them in every other way, may share the same ignorance. Yet at the end the poem comes round to the chance that, if he spent his last hours carving "for a dead grand-daughter" one of the little ivory swans that have come down to us from his people, the last of the Dorsets may have left us a thought turned into ivory and so made enduring as long as man survives to see and interpret it. As Malraux argued more elaborately, there is a way in which through art man can evade the extinction that over-takes his body and his mind.

After 600 years
the ivory thought
is still warm.

His dream of history, and his constant transfiguration of thing into myth, does not mean that Purdy's grasp is circumscribed by Canadian frontiers of time or space. Indeed, he shows the maturity of his vision by allowing it to flow freely beyond the passionate nucleus, and so, when he crosses the Divide (and he is perhaps the only eastern Canadian poet to live as comfortably on one side as on the other) and sees the cowboys riding into a little Cariboo town and their horses hitched outside the taverns, he recognizes them for what they in fact are:

...only horse and rider...
clopping into silence under the toy mountains
dropping sometimes and
                    lost in the dry grass
                    golden oranges of dung

But the horses have already set him meditating on the past of the region, the Indian past, and then he remembers the horses of history, of mythology, sweeping over a lost ancient world, and sees in fine Spenderian phrases

the ghosts of horses battering thru the wind
whose names were the wind's common usage
whose life was the sun's...

And though the poem ends in the anti-climax—the slump into existential reality—that Purdy often practises, with the thought of the Cariboo horses waiting outside the grocer's in the stink of gasoline, he has left in our minds an ineradicable image of the horse as the symbol of wild freedom in a world that man is fatally subduing and destroying.

Perhaps the most developed treatment of history as process, of man's fate to shape and be shaped, of his dual role as victor and victim, appears in Purdy's poems on Cuba, which he visited in 1964 and which filled his mind with ambivalent perturbations. It is too facile to class Purdy, as some writers have done, as merely an admirer of Castro and of Che Guevara. He admires them as men, yes, as enthusiasts fired by visions that raised them above ordinary humanity and led them to perform extraordinary tasks. But he sees clearly the trap action led them into. Castro delivers the kind of oration any other dictator might deliver; Che has a politician's handshake; and when Purdy talks in a Havana bar with Red Chinese sailors he sees the whole Cuban setting as a kind of unreal Graham Greene-ish world whose strangeness is emphasised by the inconsequential memories of an Ontario childhood that come into mind as he stands there. Yet tragedy, he insists, restores such men to humanity, and even if we cannot know the final consequences of "Che's enormous dream", the poet, thinking of his death, of his fingers cut off to indentify the prints, can

> ...remember his quick hard handshake
> in Havana among the tiny Vietnamese ladies
> and seem to hold ghostlike in my own hand
> five bloody fingers
> of Che Guevara

Anyone who has followed Purdy's writing for a long time will be aware that he is not only wide in thought and subtle in vision, but also extremely versatile as a poetic craftsman who has worked his way through the forms and styles to his present open manner. Poets nowadays seem to be divided into the short-liners and the long-liners, the halting and the fluent, roughly corresponding to the discontinuous thinkers (who are usually also the eternal-moment-men) and the linear thinkers who as Purdy is—tend also to be the historical poets. It is in the way he can manipulate the long line to create a variety of moods that Purdy has shown his growing power to fit the form exactly to the thought and thing, which is the sign of ultimate poetic craftsmanship. This is not to say that his poems are entirely linear in their overall structure, for often the juxtaposition of jarring or contrasting elements is an essential part of the effect he is seeking, and there are times when he uses the moderately short line very effectively to achieve a cumulative emotive effect.

> ...tho we keep on running
> past the Land of Flat Stones
> over the Marvel-Strands
> beyond the country of great trees...
> Tho we ran to the edge of the world,
> our masters would track us down –

But he is never one of your gasping, grunting, three-or-four-syllable-a-line men. No discursive, philosophic, historic, didactic poet–and Purdy is all these–ever can be.

Yet for all its didacticism, there is much in Purdy's poetry that has the effortless, gratuitous magic which has been the sign of a good poet in any age: lines like

> We live with death but it's life we die with
> in the blossoming earth where springs the rose...

or the whole of "Necropsy of Love", whose last lines have the kind of hypnotic midnight power of some of Keats or some Decadent poetry (compliment returned!):

If death shall strip our bones of all but bones,
then here's the flesh, and flesh that's drunken-sweet
as wine cups in deceptive lunar light:
reach up your hand and turn the moonlight off,
and maybe it was never there at all,
so never promise anything to me:
but reach across the darkness with your hand,
reach across the distance of tonight,
and touch the moving moment once again
           before you fall asleep...

There is not enough time and space here to consider the various poetic devices to which, having abandoned rhyme and ordinary metre, Purdy has recourse on the appropriate occasion: it is enough to point out, and leave the reader to find his own examples, the use of alliteration and repetition, the presence at time of regular syllabic patterns, the occasional resort to galloping trochaic rhythms, and, as a matter of rhythm as well as language, a superb colloquial ear.

Finally, after having said so much of Purdy as the history-conscious poet, the philosophizer on the human condition, the geographer of the imagination, one is suddenly aware of a noisy fellow dragging at one's legs under the impression they are wild-grape vines, and Purdy pulls one down to the earth on which, however high his head and wide his scope, his feet are surely set. For he is also the poet of comedy: picture post card domestic comedy with nagging wives and blundering husbands; high low comedy as when the poet makes a mock epic out of trying to defecate in the presence of Eskimo huskies hungry for human excrement; original Dionysiac comedy in that wild drunken poem, "The Winemaker's Beat-Étude". It is comedy that easily runs black, for it is based on a totally realistic sense of what individual man's fate is in a world where grandeur is a feat of the imagination; where man grows old though his lusts stay young; where his actions are contemptible though his thoughts are high; where his attempts to reconcile the animal and the human within him always end in comic absurdity. The decay and death that finally await him Purdy portrays with realistic horror, yet with compassion for the defeated, and with admiration for those who cry out in rage against the destiny that makes an old woman die, as in the grim poem "Evergreen Cemetery", stuffing her false teeth up her rectum. "Old Alex", an elegy on a venomous old man, is by way of an antidote to some of the nobler thoughts Purdy has dwelt on, yet it is also a sign of the universality of his sympathy, since what in the end it projects is the paradox of sublimity realized in meanness:

I don't mourn. Nobody does. Like mourning an ulcer.
Why commemorate disease in a poem then?
I don't know. But this hate was lovely,
given freely and without stint. His smallness
had the quality of making everyone else feel noble,

and thus fools. I search desperately
for good qualities, and end up crawling
inside that decaying head and wattled throat
to scream obscenities like papal blessings,
knowing now and again I'm at least God.
Well, who remembers a small purple and yellow bruise long?
But when he was here he was a sunset!

George Woodcock.

THE ROAD TO NEWFOUNDLAND

My foot has pushed a fire ahead of me
for a thousand miles
my arms' response to hills and stones
has stated parallel green curves
deep in my unknown country
the clatter of gravel on fenders registers
on a ghostly player piano
inside my head with harsh fraying music
I'm lost to reality
but turn the steering wheel a quarter
inch to avoid a bug on the road
A long time's way here since stone
age man carried the fire-germ
in a moss-lined basket
from camp to camp
and prayed to it
as I shall solemnly hold Henry Ford
and all his descendants accountable
to the 24,000 mile guarantee
Well there are many miles left
before it expires and several
more to the next rest
stop and I kick the fire
ahead of me with one foot
even harder than before
hearing the sound of burning
forests muffled in steel
toppling buildings
history accelerating
racing up and down
hills with my flesh grown captive
of a steel extension of myself
hauling down the sun and stars
for mileposts going nowhere fast
wanting speed and more Speed

–Stop
at a calm lake
embossed with 2-inch waves
sit there a few minutes
without getting out of the car
my heart a hammering drum
among the trees' and grass roots'
August diminuendo
watching the composed landscape
the sun where it's supposed to be
in its deliberate dance thru space
then drive steadily north
with the captive fire
in cool evening
towards the next camp

OVER THE HILLS IN THE RAIN, MY DEAR

We are walking back from the Viking site,
dating ten centuries ago
(it must be about four miles),
and rain beats on us,
soaks our clothes,
runs into our shoes,
makes white pleats in our skin,
turns hair into decayed seaweed:
and I think sourly that drowning
on land is a helluva slow way to die.
I walk faster than my wife,
then have to stop and wait for her:
"It isn't much farther,"
I say encouragingly,
and note that our married life
is about to end in violence,
judging from her expressionless expression.
Again I slop into the lead,
then wait in the mud till she catches up,
thinking, okay, I'll say something complimentary:

"You sure are a sexy lookin mermaid dear!"
That don't go down so good either,
and she glares at me like a female vampire
resisting temptation badly:
at which point I've forgotten
all about the rain,
trying to manufacture
a verbal comfort station,
a waterproof two-seater.
We squelch miserably into camp
about half an hour later,
strip down like white shrivelled slugs,
waving snail horns at each other,
cold sexless antennae
assessing the other ridiculous creature–
And I begin to realize
one can't use a grin like a bandaid
or antidote for reality,
at least not all the time:
and maybe it hurts my vanity
to know she feels sorry for me,
she's sorry for *me*,
and I don't know why:
but to be a fool
is sometimes
my own good luck.

L'Anse aux Meadows, Nfld.

THE RUNNERS

'It was when Leif was with King Olaf Tryggvason, and he bade him proclaim Christianity to Greenland, that the king gave him two Gaels; the man's name was Haki, and the woman's Haekia. The King advised Leif to have recourse to these people, if he should stand in need of fleetness, for they were swifter than deer. Erick and Leif had tendered Karlsefni the services of this couple. Now when they had sailed past Marvel-Strands (to the New World) they put the Gaels ashore, and directed them to run to the southward, and investigate the nature of the country, and return again before the end of the third half-day.'

From Erick the Red's Saga

Brother, the wind of this place is cold,
and hills under our feet tremble,
the forests are making magic against us—
I think the land knows we are here,
I think the land knows we are strangers.
Let us stay close to our friend the sea,
or cunning dwarves at the roots of darkness
shall seize and drag us down—

Sister, we must share our strength between us,
until the heat of our bodies makes a single flame:
while the moon sees only one shadow
and the sun knows only our double heartbeat,
and the rain does not come between—

Brother, I am afraid of this dark place,
I am hungry for the home islands,
and wind blowing the waves to coloured spray,
I am sick for the sun—

Sister, we must not think those thoughts again,
for three half-days have gone by,
and we must return to the ship.
If we are away longer,
the Northmen will beat us with thongs,
until we cry for death—
Why do you stare at nothing?

Brother, a cold wind touched me,
tho I stand in your arms' circle:
perhaps the Northmen's runes have found us,
the runes they carve on wood and stone.
I am afraid of this dark land,
ground mist that makes us half ghosts,
and another silence inside silence...
But there are berries and fish here,
and small animals by the sea's edge
that crouch and tremble and listen...
If we join our thoughts to the silence,
if our trails join the animal trails,
and the sun remembers what the moon forgets...
Brother, it comes to me now,
the long ship must sail without us,
we stay here–

Sister, we should die slowly,
the beasts would gnaw at our bodies,
the rains whiten our bones.
The Northmen's runes are strong magic,
the runes would track us down,
tho we keep on running
past the Land of Flat Stones
over the Marvel-Strands
beyond the country of great trees...
Tho we ran to the edge of the world,
our masters would track us down–

Brother, take my hand in your hand,
this part of ourselves between us
while we run together,
over the stones of the sea-coast,
this much of ourselves is our own:
while rain cries out against us,
and darkness swallows the evening,
and morning moves into stillness,
and mist climbs to our throats,
while we are running,
while we are running–

Sister–

THE CARIBOO HORSES

At 100 Mile House the cowboys ride in rolling
stagey cigarettes with one hand reining
half-tame bronco rebels on a morning grey as stone
—so much like riding dangerous women
      with whiskey coloured eyes—
such women as once fell dead with their lovers
with fire in their heads and slippery froth on thighs
—Beaver or Carrier women maybe or
      Blackfoot squaws far past the edge of this valley
on the other side of those two toy mountain ranges
      from the sunfierce plains beyond

But only horses
      waiting in stables
hitched at taverns
      standing at dawn
pastured outside the town with
jeeps and fords and chevvys and
busy muttering stake trucks rushing
importantly over roads of man's devising
over the safe known roads of the ranchers
families and merchants of the town
      On the high prairie
are only horse and rider
      wind in dry grass
clopping in silence under the toy mountains
dropping sometimes and
      lost in the dry grass
      golden oranges of dung

Only horses
                no stopwatch memories or palace ancestors
not Kiangs hauling undressed stone in the Nile Valley
and having stubborn Egyptian tantrums or
Onagers racing thru Hither Asia and
the last Quagga screaming in African highlands
                lost relatives of these
                whose hooves were thunder
the ghosts of horses battering thru the wind
whose names were the wind's common usage
whose life was the sun's
                arriving here at chilly noon
                in the gasoline smell of the
                dust and waiting 15 minutes
                at the grocer's

LATE RISING AT ROBLIN LAKE

All hours the day begins one may
awake at dawn with bird cries
streaking light to sound to song
to coloured silence wake with
sun stream shuttle threading thru
curtain shadows dazzling eyes at
4 p.m. and 9 p.m. and 1 a.m. one May
awake inside a moving house earthbound
by heart tick and clock beat only all
one August afternoon once why
stumbling yawning nude to front
window there on the dock
                in noon fog lit
with his own slow self-strangeness
stood a tall blue heron

                and the day began with him

THE DRUNK TANK

A man keeps hammering at the door
(he is so noisy it makes my ears ache),
yelling monotonously, "Let me outa here!"
A caged light bulb floats on the ceiling,
where a dung fly circles round and round,
and there is a greasy brown mattress,
too small for the bolted-down steel bunk;
and a high barred window permitting
fungus darkness to creep in the room's corners.
The man keeps hammering at the door
until a guard comes:
"I just happen to know the mayor in this town,"
he tells the guard,
"and it's gonna be too bad for you
if you keep me locked up here."
The guard laughs and turns away.
"It's no use," I tell my cell mate.
"Just wait until morning.
Then we'll be up in magistrate's court,
and being drunk isn't a very serious—"
"Who are you?" the man asks me.
"I don't know you—"
"I'm your friend," I say to him,
"and I've been your friend a long time.
Don't you remember?"
"I don't know you at all!" he screams.
"Stay away from me!"
"If that's the way you feel about it," I say,
and suddenly I'm not so sure as I was
—memory is a funny thing isn't it?
"Please sit down and wait until morning,"
I say to him reasonably—
Don't you think that was the right thing to say?
But he turns his back and hammers on the door:
"Guard! Guard! I want a cell by myself!
You've put a crazy man in here with me!"

He is so noisy.
And I watch him pounding on the black steel door,
a patch of sweat spreading on his back,
and his bald spot glistening–
He looks at me over his shoulder,
terrified:
and I spread my hands flat to show him
I have nothing but good intentions.
"Stay away from me! Stay away!"
He backs off into a corner shaking,
while I sit down on the bunk
to wait for morning.
And I think:
this is my friend,
I know it is my friend,
and I say to him,
"Aren't you my friend?"
But there he is at the door again,
he is so noisy....

MY GRANDFATHER TALKING—30 YEARS AGO

Not now boy not now
some other time I'll tell ya
what it was like
the way it was
without no streets
or names of places here
nothin but moonlight boy
nothin but woods

Why ain't there woods no more?
I lived in the trees an
how far was anywhere was
as far as the trees went
ceptin cities
            an I never went

They put a road there
where the trees was
an a girl on the road
in a blue dress
an given a place to go
from I went
into the woods with her
it bein the best way
to go an never get there

Walk in the woods an not get lost
wherever the woods go
a house in the way
a wall in the way
a stone in the way
that got there quick as hell
an a man shouting Stop
but you don't dast stop
or everything would fall down
You low it's time boy
when you can't tell anyone
when there ain't none to tell
about whatever it was I was sayin
what I was talkin about
what I was thinkin of—?

OLD ALEX

"85 years old, that miserable alcoholic
old bastard is never gonna die," the man said
where he got bed and board. But he did.
I'll say this for Alex' immortality tho:
if they dig him up in a thousand years,
and push a spigot into his belly why
his fierce cackle'll drive a nail in silence,
his laugh split cordwood and trees kow-tow
like green butlers, the staggering world
get drunk and sober men run scared.
So you say: was I fond of him?
No–not exactly anyhow. Once
he told his sons and daughters to bugger off,
and then vomited on their memory. It'd be
like liking toadstools or a gun pointing at you–
He sat home three weeks drinking whiskey,
singing harsh songs and quoting verse and chapter
from the Bible: his mean and privileged piety
dying slowly: they rolled him onto a stretcher
like an old pig and prettied him with cosmetics,
sucked his blood out with a machine and
dumped him into the ground like garbage.

I don't mourn. Nobody does. Like mourning an ulcer.
Why commemorate disease in a poem then?
I don't know. But his hate was lovely,
given freely and without stint. His smallness
had the quality of making everyone else feel noble,
and thus fools. I search desperately
for good qualities, and end up crawling
inside that decaying head and wattled throat
to scream obscenities like papal blessings,
knowing now and again I'm at least God.
Well, who remembers a small purple and yellow bruise long?
But when he was here he was a sunset!

SPRING SONG

Old father me
in the classic rural tradition
listening to frogs
larrup loopholes in silence
making sexual abstinence the ultimate
blasphemy
Rabbits turn annoyed
having shit on the garbage all winter
in near privacy
they dislike this noisy interruption
and skitter into the willows
Crying birds of passage
are overheard in the clouds plotting
a better world for starlings
Old father me
doing pushups under an ancient Pontiac
attempting to change the oil

Include me out of it all?
Never not
            so long as the farm girl has
my two soft-boiled eyes twinkling hard
against her jiggling jelly buttocks swaying
down the lane to the mailbox
wearing shorts in figleaf weather
I'm obscurely gratified but rueful too
            at the young man's vehement twitching
lechery
            inside an old man's
            voyeur-masochistic morals
under a senile Pontiac in the butter-yellow
sunlight attempting to change the oil

You bedamned you
professionally unhappy philosophers
second-hand disciples of sad old Nietzsche
or parroting McLuhan's new toilet training
followers only
            followers of anyone

not alive whether
under or above ground those
sick creators of non-human science
atomic midwives of doomgirls ending
with two heads say and four buttocks wriggling
slithering down the lane to the mailbox which
is much too much of a good thing for
a man who can't make up his mind anyway
even upside down under a ton of metal such
permutations keep an old man on his toes

The world's pain is a little away from here
and the hawk's burst of speed that claws
a fish from its glass house is earlier
and later than now under a rejuvenated
Pontiac with frogs booming temporary
sonatas for mortals and Beethoven
crows thronging the June skies and
everything still
                    everything suddenly goddam still
with the sun a hovering golden bird
                    nothing moves
                    soft clouds wait
like floating houses in the sky
and the storm beyond the horizon waiting
the planets stopped in their tracks
high over the village of Ameliasburg
                    as if forever was now
                    and the grass roots knew it all
–But they don't know you know and here I am
                    with both hands high
under the skirts of the world
trying to figure it out too late for
someone breathed or sighed or spoke
and everything rearranged itself
from is to was the white moon tracks
her silver self across the purple night
replacing earth time with a celestial
hour glass halfway between a girl
and woman I forgot till she comes jiggling
back from the dark mailbox at last migawd
hosannah in the lowest mons veneris I
will never get to change the goddam oil

ONE RURAL WINTER

Trapped
     abandoned
          marooned
like a city thief in a country jail
bitching about all the fresh air
the rural mail my only communication with outside
surrounded by nothing
          but beautiful trees
          and I hate beautiful trees
I'm lost beyond even the remote boundaries
of Ameliasburg
          and I ask you
what could be more remote than a burg
named after a German dumpling named Amelia?
Why just close your eyes tight shut here
and you don't see little dots of light
          –you see fresh cowpads
But it's winter now
          beyond the economic wall
(I have two nickels a dime and quarter
and not a damn cent
in my pockets but a wife
who comes out at night when I'm asleep
and won't meet the burning stare
of my closed dreaming womanless eyes
not for two nickels a dime and quarter anyway)

          In the backyard
phallic pieces of wood and stones embedded
in ice (notice the Freudian terminology please)
a failed writer I'm trapped forever
in the 3rd Post-Atomic Pre-Literate Glacial Period
(making witty remarks like "Cold out, ain't it Zeke?")
It's got so I'm even afraid to go outside
in order to experience the rich rural experience
that is part of our common Canadian heritage
I might catch my foot in a lateral moraine or something
and be trapped forever
          in Ameliasburg Township

The earth is frozen
the beautiful trees are frozen
even the mailbox's metal nose is cold
and I'm getting a little chilly myself
living in a house I built one tropical summer
with Unemployment Insurance money
                              and a bad-tempered wife
But I got into this mess myself
and I ain't blamin the Class Struggle
besides things are gonna get better
—in ten or twenty years I think

It does improve my character
                    no doubt of that
to walk half a mile to the outdoor shithouse
with the temperature at 40 below
But Maclean's Magazine is absorbing toilet tissue
and all the spiders and microbes and things
I trained last summer to sit up and chant
in unison Hallelujah What a Bum
                    to visiting imaginary females
from the neighbouring seminary
                    —are frozen stiff
But the place is warm and comfortable
despite the perfumed gale below
as long as you can keep your mind
                    on the beautiful girl
tacked on the wall who advises that
                    SPRING IS HERE
and I should have my crankcase flushed out
Then wiped and buttoned and zippered
I plunge back to the house
thru a white world of nothing
                    but snow
                    and the damn WIND
steals all my internal heat
it howls like a dog in my summer underwear
my heavy body is doped with wind and cold
                    and the house door
                    drags me into the hall
                    and the door knob
                    is a handle
I hold onto the sky with

WINTER AT ROBLIN LAKE

Seeing the sky darken & the fields
turn brown & the lake lead-grey
as some enormous scrap of sheet metal
& wind grabs the world around the equator
I am most thankful then for knowing about
         the little gold hairs on your belly

ROBLIN'S MILLS (1)

The mill was torn down last year
and stone's internal grey light
gives way to new green
a shading of surface colour
like the greenest apple of several
The spate of Marthas and Tabithas
         incessant Hirams and Josephs
is stemmed in the valley graveyard
where the censored quarrels of loving
and the hatred and by golly gusto
of a good crop of buckwheat and turnips
end naturally as an agreement between friends
         (in the sandy soil
that would grow nothing but weeds
or feed a few gaunt cattle)–
And the spring rain takes their bodies
a little deeper down each year
         and maybe the earliest settlers
some stern Martha or speechless Joseph
perhaps meet and mingle
         1,000 feet down–

And the story about the grist mill
rented in 1914 to a man named Taylor
by the last of the Roblin family
who demanded a share of the profits
that poured golden thru the flume
because the new miller knew his business:
        & the lighting alters
        here and now changes
to then and you can see
        how a bald man stood
sturdily indignant
        and spat on the floor
and stamped away so hard the flour
dust floated out from his clothes
like a white ghostly nimbus
around the red scorn
and the mill closed down—

        Those old ones
you can hear them on a rural party line
sometimes
        when the copper wires
sing before the number is dialed and
then your own words stall some distance
from the house you said them in
        lost in the 4th concession
        or dimension of wherever
        what happened still happens
        a lump in your throat
        an adam's apple half
        a mile down the road
        permits their voices
        to join living voices
        and float by
        on the party line sometimes
        and you hang up then
        so long now—

DARK LANDSCAPE

For a week the flies have been terrible
not medium size houseflies
but heavy foreboding buzzard-creatures
dive-bombing thru clouds of insecticide
knocking dishes from shelves
and body checking the furniture
Lying awake in darkness I hear them
blundering thru night's frontiers
frantic about something
antennae picking up signals outside the house
as if there was a point to existence
other than personal
as if they registered a protest
No sun or wind on the grey lake
all morning and thru the long afternoon
summer cottagers gone
a pair of tall elms
dead long since from dutch elm disease
are indistinguishable from other trees
their small bones leafless
Well I've no doubt weather
does influence human mood and
when it rains people are seldom optimists
in middle age the body itself
slows to contemplate nothingness
seasonal metrics stagger and jerk to a halt
mandolins in grass roots end
winter is coming
I sit stupefied
waiting ...
Across the sky a flight of geese
goes sweeping to the continental vanishing point
sends a honking cry down here now
fading to an almost inaudible mockery
as they reach toward lands of the sun
All this brings on an opposite reaction
the old man glimpses himself in a mirror
and I laugh I must laugh
it's too pat too trite and too goddam soon
too easy to turn down the music and wait
or alternatively

brush reality aside with physical action?
But "to live a life is not to cross a field"?
Is it then to cross many fields
wear blinkers and cultivate a cheerful outlook?
With brain relinquished the body takes over?
And I laugh and span the continent with a letter
write a dozen letters to Vancouver
Vancouver   Montreal   and Toronto
drink a glass of wine and knock the bottle over
down the dregs and stain my guts with purple
think about a girl who couldn't love me
(oh impossible and inconceivable to love you
as she passionately mentioned) and I laugh
and think–for life to have a meaning
or even several meanings well it's funny
tho one of them is getting rather drunken
in the afterbirth of youth and maybe wine and
maybe spring comes on forever spring goes on forever
said Aladdin to the jinn jinn gin
And maybe down below the lowest floorboards
where the dead flies buzz and blunder
a girl will whisper maybe yes I do
yes I do you euphemistic bastard
me as shouldn't me as oughtn't on accounta
you don't take women serious as you really
ought to do you
don't take livin serious
                    Yes I do yes I do
tho I'm gettin rather elderly for crossin fields in winter
is serious as anything and hemispheres take longer
and elms are dying momently as I say this to you
        and flies are something terrible
        and mushroom clouds likewise
        and there's them that die of livin
        and there's them that joy in dyin
        and there's agony and screamin
        and all I have is laughter
        all I have is wine and laughter
        and the spring came on forever
        the spring comes on forever
                    Yes I do

                Roblin Lake

37

INTERRUPTION

When the new house was built
callers came:
black squirrels on the roof every morning
between sleep and wakefulness,
and a voice saying "Hello dead man."
A chipmunk looks in the window
and I look out,
the small face and the large one
waver together in glass,
but neither moves
while the leaves turn into shadows.
Orioles, robins and red-winged blackbirds
are crayons that colour the air;
something sad and old
cries down in the swamp.
Moonlight in the living room,
a row of mice single file
route marching across the empty lunar plain
until they touch one of my thoughts
and jump back frightened,
but I don't wake up.
Pike in the lake pass and re-pass the windows
with clouds in their mouth.
For 20 minutes every night
the sun slaps a red paint brush
over dinner dishes and leftovers,
but we keep washing it off.
Birds can't take a shortcut home
they have to fly around the new house;
and cedars grow pale green candles
to light their way thru the dark.
Already the house is old:
a drowned chipmunk (the same one?)
in the rain barrel this morning,
dead robins in the roof overhang,
and the mice are terrified—
We have set traps,
and must always remember
to avoid them ourselves.

IDIOT'S SONG

Give me peace from you
allow me to go on
and be what I was before you
if there was ever that time

But talk to me talk to me
or die soon before I do
I'll come where your body is
tho it answers me nothing

But don't die
stay with me in the same world
or I'm lost and desolate
for here the light and dark
that touches you   touches   me
that you are here at all
delays my own death
an instant longer

MY GRANDFATHER'S COUNTRY
(Upper Hastings County)

Highway 62
in red October
where the Canadian shield hikes north
with southern birds gone now
Thru towns named for an English novel
a battle in Scotland and Raleigh's dream of gold
—Ivanhoe   Bannockburn   El Dorado
with "Prepare to Meet Thy God" on granite billboards
Light thru the car window
drapes the seat with silken yard goods
and over rock hills in my grandfather's country
where poplar   birch   and elm trees
are yellow as blazing lemons
the maple and oak are red as red
as the open mouth of a dinosaur
            that died for love
of eating

Of course other things are also marvellous
sunsets happen if the atmospheric conditions are right
and the same goes for a blue sky
—there are deserts like great yellow beds of flowers
where a man can walk and walk into identical distance
like an arrow lost in its own target
and a woman scream and a grain of sand will fall
on the other side of the yellow bowl a thousand miles away
and all day long like a wedge of obstinate silver
the moon is tempered and forged in yellow fire
it hangs beside a yellow sun and will not go down

And there are seas in the north so blue
that a polar bear can climb his own wish and walk the sky
and wave on wave of that high blue washes over the mind
and sings to each component part of the hearing blood
a radiance that burns down the dark buildings of night
and shines for 24 hours a day of long sea-days
and is held trembling in a bubble of memory
to remember summer by
when the white pause begins

But the hill-red has no such violence of endings
the woods are alive
and gentle as well as cruel
unlike sand and sea
and if I must commit myself to love
for any one thing
it will be here in the red glow
where failed farms sink back into earth
the clearings join and fences no longer divide
where the running animals gather their bodies together
and pour themselves upward
into the tips of falling leaves
with mindless faith that presumes a future
Earth that has discarded so much so long
over the absentminded centuries
has remembered the protein formula
from the invincible mould
the chemicals that after selection select themselves
the muscles that kill and the nerves that twitch and rage
the mind-light assigned no definite meaning
but self-regarding and product of the brain
an inside room where the files are kept
and a little lamp of intelligence burns sometimes
with flickering irritation that it exists at all
that occasionally conceives what it cannot conceive
itself and the function of itself:
narrowing the problem down to a deaf mute in a wind tunnel
narrowing the problem down to a blind man in a hall of mirrors
narrowing the problem down—

Day goes as if someone had closed their eyes
or a non-existent god was thinking of something else
night comes black velvet and the red glow fades
leaves fall in my grandfather's country
and mine too for that matter
then day returns horizontal and gloomy again
leaves fall in the rain-coloured light
exposing for ornithologists here and there
in the future
some empty waiting birds' nests

MARRIED MAN'S SONG

When he makes love to the young girl
what does the middleaged long-married
man say to himself and the girl?
—that lovers live and desk clerks perish?

When neons flash the girl into light and shadow
the room vanishes and all those others
guests who checked out long ago
are smiling
and only the darkness of her may be touched
only the whiteness looked at
she stands above him as a stone goddess
weeping tears and honey
she is half his age and far older
and how can a man tell his wife this?

Later they'll meet in all politeness
not quite strangers but never friends
and hands touched elsewhere may shake together
with brush of fingers and casual eyes
and the cleanser cleans to magic whiteness
and love survives in the worst cologne
(but not girls' bodies that turn black leather)
for all believe in the admen's lies

In rare cases among the legions of married men
such moments of shining have never happened
and whether to praise such men for their steadfast virtue
or condemn them as fools for living without magic
answer can hardly be given

There are rooms for rent in the outer planets
and neons blaze in Floral Sask
we live with death but it's life we die with
in the blossoming earth where springs the rose
In house and highway in town and country
what's given is paid for blood gifts are sold
the stars' white fingers unscrew the light bulbs
the bill is due and the desk clerk wakes
outside our door the steps are quiet
light comes and goes from a ghostly sun
where only the darkness may be remembered
and the rest is gone

PERCY LAWSON
(Contract Negotiator–Vancouver Upholsterers' Union)

Sitting with Lawson in 1954
        sitting with Percy Lawson
ill at ease in the boss's panelled office
after work hours talking of nothing
talking of practically almost nothing
a lousy nickel raise that is
        haggling over a lousy nickel
and maybe besides the long and hourly
bearable toil of an almost lifetime
(East Indians: 35 years
        Canadians: 70–figures approximate)
Listen in again in the boss's panelled office
        listen to Lawson
listen to Percy Lawson
–thinking of girls in the cutting room
afraid of the union
        afraid for their jobs and
thinking of me–afraid of Watt or
not afraid
        only wanting to be liked
and knowing for sure I'm not
Thinking of Lawson
        up from the coal mines
on the island and gotten fat
since talking and haggling and
being afraid of practically nothing
but death and his wife and damn near
        everything but not
bosses
not Watt
And what's the contract news from Watt who
if I said what I thought he was would
sue me for damn near everything
would sue me right now in a poem and
get a judgment for one lying lyric
        I can't write
        (I'll be damned if I write)
in praise of Watt
in praise of
        practically nothing

But I listen to Percy Lawson
    haggling over a lousy nickel
listen to the sonuvabitch
    haggling over a lousy nickel
the twentieth part of a dollar that
    winks among the words
like a clean magician's coin
born from virginal nothing and not
mined or smelted and sweated and laboured for for
the twentieth part of a wasted hour back there
in the silvery guts of a labouring terribly useful lifetime
In a tactical pause between the chop
    of words Lawson turns
the little fat man probably dead now
    turns then
and gives me a gold-toothed grin

.

NOTES ON A FICTIONAL CHARACTER

With cobwebs between elbows and knees,
I say that I hate violence:
there have been street fights;
two wills glaring eye to eye arm
wrestling–;
hours struggling for my soul or hers
with a woman in a taxi;
whacked and bloody and beaten in a poolroom,
playing pool with the winner and winning,
then the walk home, and fall down like a broken chair,
that kind of pride.
All violence,
the inner silent implacable defiance
of money or god or damn near anything:
but it was useful once
to the middle-aged man with belly and ballpoint
getting drunk on words but sobering ah sobering.
Remember the factory manager Arthur Watt,
big, charming smile, attractive personality,
who worked alongside his crew,
wearing a white shirt and tailored trousers,
to increase production:
one day Watt and four others
pulled against three of us across a table,
hauling the cover onto a mattress
much too big for the cover, with ropes,
a workday job delightfully turned to a tug-o-war:
me, digging up more strength than I had,
aimed it at Watt especially,
yanked the bastard toward me,
dragged an extra ten pounds of myself
from the guts and yanked
the boss till his head banged wood with
both arms stretched toward me on the table praying
to Allah there is no god but Allah
                              W. Purdy...

The trick was to keep an absolutely straight face,
no expression whatever hold
the chortle to a goddam whimper
of pure joy that started in the balls
and raced 90-miles-per-hour to the angels' antennae
where it sang sweet songs to female cherubs
emerging in the factory dust as a deprecating tsk-tsk,
a normal cigarette cough,
successfully dishonestly solicitous.
As a matter of course he hated me,
which I accepted modestly as my just due:
I've drawn it after me down the years,
that sobbing violence,
ropes to the mattress past like cobwebs
that break with a sudden movement or gentle smile:
or, tough as steel hawsers,
the ropes drag me inch by inch
to the other side of the table,
where the factory manager waits
his unruly workman with a gun,
to watch with amazed eyes
while I write this poem,
like blossoming thistle.

HOME-MADE BEER

I was justly annoyed 10 years ago
in Vancouver: making beer in a crock
under the kitchen table when this
next door youngster playing with my own
kid managed to sit down in it and
emerged with one end malted—
With excessive moderation I yodelled
at him
          "Keep your ass out of my beer!"
          and the little monster fled—
Whereupon my wife appeared from the bathroom
where she had been brooding for days
over the injustice of being a woman and
attacked me with a broom—
With commendable savoir faire I broke
the broom across my knee (it hurt too) and
then she grabbed the breadknife and made
for me with fairly obvious intentions—
I tore open my shirt and told her calmly
with bared breast and a minimum of boredom
          "Go ahead! Strike! Go ahead!"
Icicles dropped from her fiery eyes as she
snarled
          "I wouldn't want to go to jail
          for killing a thing like you!"
I could see at once that she loved me
tho it was cleverly concealed—
For the next few weeks I had to distribute
the meals she prepared among neighbouring
dogs because of the rat poison and
addressed her as Missus Borgia—
That was a long time ago and while
at the time I deplored her lack of
self control I find myself sentimental
about it now for it can never happen again—

Sept. 22, 1964: P.S., I was wrong—

DYLAN

I read him on the bus going
back and forth to work
in Vancouver in 1954
getting my feet stepped on
in a parable of green chapels told
to move on back in the car
by a critical conductor
and girls like Hansel and Gretel
maybe but not Caitlin gave me
some dirty looks and a glare
on Clarke Drive and Hastings East
reading Dylan over and over
till I didn't understand much better
and standing in Kingsway rain
queueing up forever and ever and
the force that thru the green fuse
is liable to get the straphanger's face slapped
looking down the front of girls' dresses
and he gets off at the wrong stop
and goes to work in the wrong factory
and one of us is living the wrong lifetime
which is neither here nor there of course
without understanding in the least
at best a little drunk
with time and words not knowing
any good reason for Vancouver
in 1954

FIDEL CASTRO IN REVOLUTIONARY SQUARE

He begins to speak
about guns and drums and sugar
production higher this year
(a million people listening)
about impossible peace
and war and I wonder
how it was
with that young student
years ago in Havana drinking
with friends silently the colour
of Cuban April on his face
from flowers and the red earth
outside fading in the gold afternoon
I wonder about that young student
and speculate the exact moment
he sprang to his feet
stuttering with earnestness:
      "Listen to me:
        we're going to take over
        all of us here in this room
        the people here in this room
        and all the people
        we're going to take over the country"
The fragile intention flees
from face to face like fever
becomes a condition of existence
a thought to think when first
putting on your pants in the morning
and the faces gather around him
the whispering ghosts of justice
say to him "Fidel! Fidel!?"
and the high talk begins
And a stranger sits down then
shaken and sweating
not the same young student
not the same man
Ten years and three hours
later in 1964
the long speech ends
and it's "Fidel! Fidel!"
without any question at all

Everyone joins hands and sings together
a million voices and bodies
sway back and forth in the sunlight
and make some remark about being human
addressed to no one exactly
spoken to no imperialist
snarled at no invader
as natural as eating supper
that is able to touch the future
and fill an emptiness
and fills an emptiness in the future
Or else that's another illusion
something nice to believe in
and all of us need something
something to lift us from ourselves
a thing we touch that touches
a future we don't know
the continuity of people
a we/they and me/you concept
as saccharine as religion
to comfort a world of children
with proletarian lullabies
A million people move to the exits
under a sky empty of everything
returning to the fact of duration
and chicken hearts in nutritive solution
and glands living the good life
                        in a test tube
the great ambiguity the last cliché
And back at the shining Cadillac
we came in (Batista's old car)
under the side where I hadn't
noticed before the body
of a small dead animal

                Cuba

HOMBRE

–Met briefly in Havana
among the million Cubans waiting
Fidel's speech on May Day 1964
under a million merciless suns
He came around and shook hands
with the foreign visitors
a guy who looked like a service station attendant
in his olive drab fatigues and beret
but with the beard and black cigar
the resemblance ended
–the Argentine doctor and freedom fighter
Che Guevara
And I remember thinking the North Vietnamese ladies
looked especially flower-like beside him
I remember his grip particularly
firm but perfunctory
half politician and half revolutionary
for he had many hands to shake that day

Later he disappeared from Cuba
and there were rumours of quarrels
between himself and Castro
and U.S. newspapers asked nervously
"Where is Che Guevara?"
And some thought he might turn up
in the American South to lead the Negroes
and march with a black army to the sea
over the green hills and racist cities
But Havana Radio reported Guevara
had joined guerillas in "a South American country"
spreading the doctrine of world revolution
in accordance with recognized medical practice
And the U.S. expressed some small doubt
about the reliability of Havana Radio
while I thought of him–shaking hands

Back home in Canada I remembered Guevara
along with structural details of Cuban girls
the Grand Hotel at Camaguay with roosters
yammering into my early morning sleep
an all-night walk in Havana streets with a friend
a mad jeep-ride over the Sierra Maestras
where sea-raiders attacked a coastal sugar mill
and Playa Giron which is the "Bay of Pigs"
where the dead men have stopped caring
and alligators hiss in the late afternoon
Again May Day in Havana 1964
with a red blaze of flowers and banners
and Castro talking solemnly to his nation
a million people holding hands and singing
strange to think of this in Canada
And I remember Che Guevara
a man who made dreams something
he could hold in his hands both hands
saying "Hiya" or whatever they say in Spanish
to the flower-like Vietnamese ladies
cigar tilted into his own trademark
of the day when rebels swarmed out
of Oriente Province down from the mountains

"Where is Che Guevara?" is answered:
deep in Bolivian jungles leading his guerillas
from cave to cave with scarlet cockatoos screaming
the Internationale around his shoulders
smoking a black cigar and wearing a beret
(like a student in Paris on a Guggenheim)
his men crawling under hundred foot trees
where giant snakes mate in masses of roots
and men with infected wounds moan for water
while Guevara leads his men into an ambush
and out again just like in the movies
but the good guy loses and the bad guys always win
and the band plays the Star-Spangled Banner

Well it is over
Guevara is dead now and whether the world
is any closer to freedom because
of Che's enormous dream is not to be known
the bearded Argentine doctor who translated
that dream to a handshake among Bolivian peasants
and gave himself away free to those who wanted him
his total self and didn't keep any
I remember the news reports from Bolivia
how he was wounded   captured   executed   cremated
but first they cut off his fingers
for fingerprint identification later
in case questions should be asked
and I remember his quick hard handshake
in Havana among the tiny Vietnamese ladies
and seem to hold ghostlike in my own hand
five bloody fingers
of Che Guevara

DREAM OF HAVANA

Talking to Red Chinese sailors
with a Cuban interpreter
at the bar in a dark night club
and so hot the air is thick
you have to move sideways & backward
in order to go forward
I listen to inscrutable orientals
stunned by Chinese vowels
Outside on the waterfront
anti-aircraft guns aim at the sky
searchlights swing like jumpy nerves
awaiting the Roman invasion
a grey American warship
cruises beyond the 12-mile limit
an international ghost
waiting for buttons to be pushed
on the doorstep of the haunted sea

In the Sierra Maestras
tanks rumble over mountain roads
coconut palms tremble
Here in Havana Fidel
finds another friend's apartment
and settles himself for sleep
while his potential assassin
dials information
at the switchboard of dreams
What world is this I've come to?
I don't believe it
not for a moment
and my thoughts exit
sideways and backward
to childhood and a lost dog
tantrums and broken toys
trouble enough
and mothers in long ago
doorways calling children home
at night for bedtime
while the Red Chinese sailors
mumble in my ear
and I drink white rum
to the dreaming trombones

Cuba

SERGEANT JACKSON

In the long grass lying
there in 1944 hating
that sergeant
hating him for thinking three
stripes made him so superior
he could get away with anything
Peering thru long grass at him
while he barked orders to God
and some airmen on a clean-up job
hoping his face might alter
flush or grow pale
and he might double over with agony
from thought-force in my eyes
the do-it-yourself voodoo
hate of an L.A.C.
—trying to make the self-important
bastard throw up his dinner
contract any ailment untrivial
like a permanent dose of clap
or imaginary fleas
approx. the size of rats
A big eagle circling the sun
with eyes a golden snare
looped round the still green valley
with snow peaks overhead
dust blowing devils across the airfield
the Skeena sailing past
railways tracks heading for Rupert
Vancouver a million miles away
48-hour pass cancelled
myself stuck there forever
where even the Japs would be welcome
but they have more sense
and no woman and no women
landing here like fallen angels
All this a long time ago

I remember grass tickling my chin
mountains high and near and far away
axe blows smashing at silence
Indian canoes on the Skeena
totem poles and some friends
nothing is lost
That sergeant?
I convince no one now
even myself
that I hated him
but my hate was holy as kosher foreskins then
and life got damned interesting
a sword was laid across the month of August
and I searched all the medical books
in camp for poisonous mountain plants
it worked like LSD
and made the landscape glow
black runways where the planes landed
writhed like snakes in the heat haze
even the dirt-poor tubercular Indians
carved themselves in my mind
and made Greek sculpture seem shoddy imitation
dead marble beside strong living flesh
But no one else noticed
how the edges of things sharpened
and quivered like fine gold lettering
on the pages of cracked parchment
in the hands of a drunken monk
and the crummy barracks lit up
during poker games
and left that time photographed
in the dumb compartments of memory
where love was slowly becoming possible

ABOUT BEING A MEMBER OF OUR ARMED FORCES

Remember the early days of the phony war
when men were zombies and women were CWACs
and they used wooden rifles on the firing range?
Well I was the sort of soldier you couldn't trust
with a wooden rifle
and when they gave me a wooden bayonet
life was fraught with peril for my brave comrades
including the sergeant-instructor
I wasn't exactly a soldier tho
only a humble airman
who kept getting demoted
     and demoted
       and demoted
to the point where I finally saluted civilians
And when they trustingly gave me a Sten gun
Vancouver should have trembled in its sleep
for after I fired a whole clip of bullets
at some wild ducks under Burrard Bridge
(on guard duty at midnight)
they didn't fly away for five minutes
trying to decide if there was any danger
Not that the war was funny
I took it and myself quite seriously
the way a squirrel in a treadmill does
too close to tears for tragedy
too far from the banana peel for laughter
and I didn't blame anyone for being there
that wars happened wasn't anybody's fault then
now I think it is

ARCTIC RHODODENDRONS

They are small purple surprises
in the river's white racket
and after you've seen them
a number of times
in water-places
where their silence seems
related to river-thunder
you think of them as 'noisy flowers'
Years ago
it may have been
that lovers came this way
stopped in the outdoor hotel
to watch the water floorshow
and lying prone together
where the purged green
boils to a white heart
and the shore trembles
like a stone song
flowers were their conversation
and love the sound of a colour
that lasts two weeks in August
and then dies
except for the three or four
I pressed in a letter
and sent whispering to you

Pangnirtung

THE TURNING POINT

Over northern Canada
daylight ahead and growing
behind only darkness
at 2.30 in the morning
while the D.C.4's engines drone

Suzanne the stewardess
is a French Canadian agnostic
which surprises me a little

Then she says most of her friends
feel the same way about god
and points where the last
darkness lingers
with the moon's silver image
on the silver aircraft

"But I see angels out there sometimes"
"Human angels?" I say
She laughs and talks about going
back to U. of M. to get her M.A.
and I must have said the wrong thing

The full shape of the Arctic moves
under us and flows
into quiet islands and tilted coastlines
blue seas reflecting our tiny aeroplane
the runaway world upside down
and no god of chaos to lift one hand
and make the place behave

Then it's gone completely
we're lost
entombed in wool blankets
and go whispering thru nothingness
without sun or moon
human instruments haywire
But we find another world
a few minutes later
with snow-streaked hills down there
that must be Baffin Island

A club-shaped word
a land most unlike Cathay or Paradise
but a place the birds return to
a name I've remembered since childhood
in the first books I read
a warm kind of wonder in myself
I used to be ashamed of

It's getting cold as hell
                    here I guess
the Arctic is no place for shirtsleeves
The stewardess serves coffee before we land
and looks out the window absentmindedly
at wings buffeting the grey air
our cloud blindfold removed
"Are they still with us, Suzanne?"

Over Fort Chimo, and later at Frobisher Bay

TREES AT THE ARCTIC CIRCLE
(Salix Cordifolia–Ground Willow)

They are 18 inches long
or even less
crawling under rocks
grovelling among the lichens
bending and curling to escape
making themselves small
finding new ways to hide
Coward trees
I am angry to see them
like this
not proud of what they are
bowing to weather instead
careful of themselves
worried about the sky
afraid of exposing their limbs
like a Victorian married couple

I call to mind great Douglas firs
I see tall maples waving green
and oaks like gods in autumn gold
the whole horizon jungle dark
and I crouched under that continual night
But these
even the dwarf shrubs of Ontario
mock them
Coward trees

And yet—and yet—
their seed pods glow
like delicate grey earrings
their leaves are veined and intricate
like tiny parkas
They have about three months
to make sure the species does not die
and that's how they spend their time
unbothered by any human opinion
just digging in here and now
sending their roots down down down
And you know it occurs to me
                    about 2 feet under
those roots must touch permafrost
ice that remains ice forever
and they use it for their nourishment
they use death to remain alive

I see that I've been carried away
in my scorn of the dwarf trees
most foolish in my judgments
To take away the dignity
                    of any living thing
even tho it cannot understand
                    the scornful words
is to make life itself trivial
and yourself the Pontifex Maximus
                    of nullity
I have been stupid in a poem
I will not alter the poem
but let the stupidity remain permanent
as the trees are
in a poem
the dwarf trees of Baffin Island

                    Pangnirtung

WASHDAY

An oil drum full
of greasy water simmering
all morning with
a blubber fire
underneath
Two women dip
water into plastic tubs
then scrub by hand
with store detergent
I stand and watch
then join the scrubbing
myself
for no reason or any
I can think of
and work at the clothes
seriously as hell
And Leah laughs
her smooth broad face
convulsed with it
a small saliva bubble
blown from her lips
and even Regally
so much darker and quiet
concedes a smile
I think then
even without knowing
the language at all
it's possible to speak
to them
          dark hair falling
in Leah's eyes as
she laughs and brushes
it back giving me
washday instruction
the baby asleep
on her back

Regally impatient
at this foolery
her standing darkness
looms over me
like a small storm cloud
disapprovingly
They chatter about it
in Eskimo
and I try to figure out
what they're saying
remembering I read somewhere
how they add syllable to
syllable so
that a sentence
is just one long word
that keeps being added to
or something like that
Leah still smiling
over the crazy visitor
who wants to wash her clothes
brown eyes and
deep dimples in cheeks
she keeps talking

Suddenly I
feel I'm picked up
with surprised vertigo
and held
between those lips
as she adds my name
to the weightless sounds
breathed out
some of the 'me' I am
removed
the walled self
defenses down
altered
I'm given to the air
then back to myself
like a gift from her
On impulse
I say
        "Leah"
and stop then
but she looks at me
as if we had exchanged
something
that the language
does not contain
And wind promenades
among the tents
wrestles with canvas
and the dogs
shit around us

Kikastan Islands

THE SCULPTORS

Going thru cases and cases
of Eskimo sculpture
returned from Frobisher
because they said it wasn't
good enough for sale to
T. Eaton Co. Ltd.
Getting itchy excelsior packing
inside my shirt and searching
for one good carving
one piece that says "I AM"
to keep a southern promise
One 6-inch walrus (tusk broken)
cribbage board (ivory inlay gone)
dog that has to be labelled dog
polar bear (badly crippled)
what might be a seal (minus flipper)
and I'm getting tired of this
looking for something
not knowing what it is
But I guess they got tired too
looking for rabbit or bear
with blisters from carving tools
dime-sized and inflating
into quarters on their fingers
waiting
for walrus or white whale
under the ice floes to
flop alive on their laps
with twitching animal faces
unready to taste the
shoe blacking carvers use
for stone polish
I'm a little ashamed of myself
for being impatient with them
but there must be something

there must be something
one piece that glows
one slap-happy idiot seal
alien to the whole seal-nation
one anthropomorphic walrus
singing Hallelujah I'm a Bum
in a whiskey baritone
But they're all flawed
broken
      bent
          misshapen
failed animals
with vital parts missing
And I have a sudden vision
of the carvers themselves
in this broken sculpture
as if the time & the place & me
had clicked into brief alignment
and a switch pulled
so that I can see and feel
what it was like to be them
the tb out-patients
failed hunters
who make a noise at the wrong time
or think of something else
at the trigger moment
and shine their eyes
into a continual tomorrow
the losers and failures
who never do anything right
and never will
the unlucky ones
always on the verge
of a tremendous discovery
who finally fail to deceive
even themselves as time begins
to hover around them
the old the old the old
who carve in their own image
of maimed animals
And I'd like to buy every damn case

Pangnirtung

WHEN I SAT DOWN TO PLAY THE PIANO

He cometh forth hurriedly from his tent
and looketh for a quiet sequestered vale
he carrieth a roll of violet toilet tissue
and a forerunner goeth ahead to do him honour
yclept a snotty-nosed Eskimo kid
He findeth a quiet glade among great stones
squatteth forthwith and undoeth trousers
"The Irrational Man" by Wm. Barrett in hand
while the other dismisseth mosquitoes
and beginneth the most natural of natural functions
buttocks balanced above the boulders
Then
     dogs[1]
        Dogs[3]
           DOGS[12]
                all shapes and sizes
all colours and religious persuasion
a plague of dogs rushing in
having been attracted by the philosophic climate
and being wishful to learn about existential dogs
and denial of the self with regard to bitches
But let's call a spade a shovel
therefore there I am I am I think that is
surrounded by a dozen dozen fierce Eskimo dogs
with an inexplicable (to me) appetite
for human excrement
                 Dear Ann Landers
what would you do?
                 Dear Galloping Gourmet
what would you do
                in a case like this?
Well I'll tell you
NOT A DAMN THING
You just squat there cursing hopelessly
while the kid throws stones
and tries to keep them off and out from under
as a big black husky dashes in
swift as an enemy submarine
white teeth snapping at the anus

I shriek
        and shriek
        (the kid laughs)
        and hold onto my pants
        sans dignity
        sans intellect
        sans Wm. Barrett
        and damn near sans anus
Stand firm little Eskimo kid
it giveth candy if I had any
it giveth a dime in lieu of same
STAND FIRM
Oh avatar of Olympian excellence
noble Eskimo youth do your stuff
Zeus in the Arctic dog pound
Montcalm at Quebec
Horatius at the bridge
Leonidas at Thermopylae
Custer's last stand at Little Big Horn
"KEEP THEM DAMN DOGS OFF
YOU MISERABLE LITTLE BRAT!"

Afterwards
Achilles retreateth without honour
unzippered and sullen
and sulketh in his tent till next time appointed
his anus shrinketh
he escheweth all forms of laxative and physick meanwhile
and prayeth for constipation
addresseth himself to the Eskimo brat miscalled
        "Lo tho I walk thru the valley of
                the shadowy kennels
        in the land of permanent ice cream
                I will fear no huskies
                for thou art with me
        and slingeth thy stones forever and ever
                thou veritable David
                                Amen"
P.S. Next time I'm gonna take a gun

                    Kikastan Islands

70

LAMENT FOR THE DORSETS
(Eskimos extinct in the 14th century A.D.)

Animal bones and some mossy tent rings
scrapers and spearheads   carved ivory swans
all that remains of the Dorset giants
who drove the Vikings back to their long ships
talked to spirits of earth and water
—a picture of terrifying old men
so large they broke the backs of bears
so small they lurk behind bone rafters
in the brain of modern hunters
among good thoughts and warm things
and come out at night
to spit on the stars

The big men with clever fingers
who had no dogs and hauled their sleds
over the frozen northern oceans
awkward giants
                killers of seal
they couldn't compete with little men
who came from the west with dogs
Or else in a warm climatic cycle
the seals went back to cold waters
and the puzzled Dorsets scratched their heads
with hairy thumbs around 1350 A.D.
—couldn't figure it out
went around saying to each other
plaintively   .
            "What's wrong? What happened?
            Where are the seals gone?"
And died

Twentieth century people
apartment dwellers
executives of neon death
warmakers with things that explode
—they have never imagined us in their future
how could we imagine them in the past
squatting among the moving glaciers

71

six hundred years ago
with glowing lamps?
As remote or nearly
as the trilobites and swamps
when coal became
or the last great reptile hissed
at a mammal the size of a mouse
that squeaked and fled

Did they ever realize at all
what was happening to them?
Some old hunter with one lame leg
a bear had chewed
sitting in a caribou-skin tent
—the last Dorset?
Let's say his name was Kudluk
and watch him sitting there
carving 2-inch ivory swans
for a dead grand-daughter
taking them out of his mind
the places in his mind
where pictures are
He selects a sharp stone tool
to gouge a parallel pattern of lines
on both sides of the swan
holding it with his left hand
bearing down and transmitting
his body's weight
from brain to arm and right hand
and one of his thoughts
turns to ivory
The carving is laid aside
in beginning darkness
at the end of hunger
and after a while wind
blows down the tent and snow
begins to cover him
After 600 years
the ivory thought
is still warm

AT THE MOVIES

The setting is really unreal
about 150 Eskimos and whites
jammed into a Nissen hut to
watch Gary Cooper and Burt Lancaster
in a technicolour western shootemup
Eskimos don't understand the dialogue
at all but they like the action
and when noble Gary is in danger
or sinister Lancaster acts menacing
a tide of emotion sweeps the hot little hut
and kids crawling on the floor almost quiet
sensing what their parents feel
that something tremendously important is happening
When the Anglican minister changes reels
(his blond head glinting as he administers
spiritual unction to his flock)
cigarettes are lit and everyone talks and
a kid crawls under my legs grinning bashfully
Jim Kilabuk says something I can't quite hear
a baby cries in the pouch on his mother's back
and is joggled gently
It's hot and stuffy as hell in the theatre
doors have to be opened
the odour of white and Eskimo
making a point for air conditioning
Lights go out and Gary Cooper rides again
the forces of evil are finally defeated
only the virtuous bullet kills
violence neutralizes violence
like a mustard plaster
(tho I kinda like the bad guy)
the way it always does in American movies
with an obvious moral a clear-cut denouement
Outside the fiord looks like poured blue milk
mountains are stone temples under a cold sky
little islands are moon prisoners
where this story happens

It's 11 p.m.
some of the hunters visit their boats
where dead caribou drain into bilgewater
and the rest of the moviegoers go
home to tents on the beach or prefab houses
and dogs howl to make everything regional
But the point I'd hoped to separate
from all these factual things stubbornly
resists me and I walk home slowly feeling stupid
rejecting the obvious
threading my way between stones in the mud
with the beginnings of a headache

Pangnirtung

WHAT DO THE BIRDS THINK?

Are they exiles here from the rest of the world?
Déjà vu past egg and atom
from the yellow Sahara-ocean
or farmlands in Ontario
a witness   hanging   painted
in the rural blue
while a plowman half a mile down
in the dark field with a snoring tractor
moves in circular sleep?
Or exiles from the apple country
where Macs and Spies plop soft
on wet ground in slow autumn days
with the rotten tangy odour
of cider rising on moonwept nights?
Have they lists and a summary
of things elsewhere and
remember the crimson racket
encountering tropic strangers
or nests of an old absence
lined with a downy part of themselves
far south?
And being south do they think sometimes
of the rain and mists of Baffin
and long migrations wingtip to wingtip
a mile high
and mate to mate in the lift and tremble
of windy muscles pushing them
pushing them where?
And do they ever
an arrow leader pointing the way
touch wearily down on ships passing?
—"Rest here a while and go on!"
(Forgotten in the hurry
of their streaming generations
another captain
called Noah
& Bjarni Herjolffson
in horned helmet
and the sweeps' silver lifting
to a luring Hyperborean ocean

or whaling ships' myopic stumbling
from dull wave to dull wave and the
paint of the bright over-the-horizon-gazing
woman flaked with salt)
How are we kept here
by what bonds
are we always exiles
a chirping roar in the silence
of foxes and watery romp of walrus
in the long sea lands
or perched on rubbery muskeg
like blue teacups
or lost brown mittens
by what agency of restlessness
in the homeless heart?
Until on a day the eggs hatch
and the young are trained to endurance
ice rattles the shroud of summer
the flight plans sent
the log book sand is scribbled on
"Goodbye–we are going–Hurry"
and mounting a shaft of sunlight
or the mizzen mast of the sky
they climb and go
And that is the way it is?
Except perhaps I wonder
do they ever
remember down there in the southland
Cumberland Sound
and the white places
of Baffin
that I will remember
soon?

Pangnirtung

THE COUNTRY OF THE YOUNG

A.Y. Jackson for instance
83 years old
halfway up a mountain
standing in a patch of snow
to paint a picture that says
"Look here
  You've never seen this country
  it's not the way you thought it was
  Look again"
And boozy traders
lost in a dream of money
crews of homesick seamen
moored to a China-vision
hunting the North West Passage
they didn't see it either
The colours I mean
for they're not bright Gauguin
or blazing Vincent
not even Breughel's "Hunters in the Snow"
where you can get lost
and found in five minutes
—but the original colour-matrix
that after a giant's heartbeat
lighted the maple forests
in the country south

You have to stoop a little
bend over and then look up
–dull orange on a cliff face
that says iron deposits
olive leaves of the ground willow
with grey silver catkins
minute wild flower beacons
sea blue as the world's eye–
And you can't be looking for something else
money or a night's lodging on earth
a stepping stone to death maybe
or you'll never find the place
hear an old man's voice
in the country of the young
that says
   "Look here–"

    Pangnirtung

HELPING MY WIFE GET SUPPER

Something basically satisfying real and valid
about being a husband
brandishing a knife
and cutting up soggy tomatoes
                    not just red
but red all through
And there's something undeniably profound
                    about being red all thru
like a cavalry charge in the salad
But I could get indignant at this lettuce
for allowing itself to be sliced
by somebody's husband like so much dead meat
                    not making a move
to defend itself
just lying there limply depending on being green
Not like the onion
                    which is not defenseless
                    for nobody makes friends with an onion
                    except another one
                    and then they don't trust each other
                    like enemy skunks
And the carrot's such a bright orange orange
it ought to be more than just a carrot
which anyway is a futile condition to be in
and it might be better not to be a carrot
                    be warned beforehand
that if you persist in this kind of carrot behaviour
you're liable to be somebody's husband
                    but nobody ever is

HOUSE GUEST

For two months we quarrelled over socialism   poetry
                                        how to boil water
doing the dishes   carpentry   Russian steel production
                                        figures and whether
you could believe them and whether Toronto Leafs would
                                        take it all
that year and maybe hockey was rather like a good jazz combo
never knowing what came next
Listening
how the new house built with salvaged old lumber
bent a little in the wind and dreamt of the trees it came from
the time it was travelling thru
and the world of snow moving all night in its blowing sleep
while we discussed ultimate responsibility for a pile of dirty
                                        dishes
Jews in the Negev   the Bible as mythic literature
                                        Peking Man
and in early morning looking outside to see the pink shapes
                                        of wind
printed on snow and a red sun tumbling upward almost
                                        touching the house
and fretwork tracks of rabbits outside where the window light
                                        had lain
last night an audience
watching in wonderment the odd human argument
that uses words instead of teeth
and got bored and went away

Of course there was wild grape wine and a stove full
                                        of Douglas fir
(railway salvage) and lake ice cracking its knuckles in hard
                                        Ontario weather
and working with saw and hammer at the house all winter
                                        afternoon
disagreeing about how to pound nails
arguing vehemently over how to make good coffee
Marcus Aurelius   Spartacus   Plato and Francois Villon

And it used to frustrate him terribly
that even when I was wrong he couldn't prove it
and when I agreed with him he was always suspicious
and thought he must be wrong because I said he was right
Every night the house shook from his snoring
a great motor driving us on into daylight
and the vibration was terrible
Every morning I'd get up and say "Look at the nails—
you snored them out half an inch in the night—"
He'd believe me at first and look and get mad and glare
and stare angrily out the window while I watched 10 minutes
                    of irritation
drain from his eyes onto fields and farms and miles and miles
                    of snow

We quarrelled over how dour I was in early morning
and how cheerful he was for counterpoint
and I argued that a million years of evolution
from snarling apeman have to be traversed before noon
and the desirability of murder in a case like his
and whether the Etruscans were really Semites
the Celtic invasion of Britain   European languages
                    Roman law
we argued about white being white (prove it dammit)
                    & cockroaches
bedbugs in Montreal   separatism   Nietzsche   Iroquois
                    horsebreakers on the prairie
death of the individual and the ultimate destiny of man
and one night we quarrelled over how to cook eggs
In the morning driving to town we hardly spoke
and water poured downhill outside all day for it was spring
when we were gone with frogs mentioning lyrically
Russian steel production figures on Roblin Lake which were
                    almost nil
I left him hitch hiking on #2 Highway to Montreal
and I guess I was wrong about those eggs

COLLECTING THE SQUARE ROOT OF MINUS ONE

(Or: Stone Blood Makes Thirsty Vampires)

To owe money—this the creditors think important.
I have one eye always on the curious stranger asking questions
about me in the village store,
the other on the rural mailbox:
containing a summons most likely
(leave the damn thing be and fly to South America!);
containing a cheque for valuable services to a rich unmarried
                                    lady
(oh open it open it quickly!).
I am fascinated by the limitless possibilities,
including this definite fact: some bastard wants his money.

Broken agreements, contracts, promises, liens and mortgages,
each calling for a slight alteration of judgment of self:
every decision, word, thought, positive act,
causes the sum of the parts of a man's self to change,
and he betrays himself into the future day after uncertain day:
or else confirms the durable fiery inveterate bone into fossil virtue—
But re-appraisal after the lost lovely cut-away pound of flesh
                                    turns rotten
in the creditor's deep freeze or
he writhes on the bloody butcher's block and escapes screaming
(tells the creditor to go to hell)
makes a man nervously uncertain about the relative importance
                                    of front
and rear doorbells—

Owing money to friends is another thing:
owing favours, embarrassed smiles, small courtesies, suspended
                                    personal opinions,
each of uncertain value but payable on smiling demand:
and the puffed-up momentarily powerful friendly creditor annuls
and invalidates all handshakes with notes to hand—

However,
flattery involves me happily in all this attention,
that a creditor should think so valuable something it's possible
                    for me to have–
I'm glad to agree that the amount of the debt is worth much
                    more than I am:
he thinks it has more value than the star-filled galaxy
(gold of the fabled Indies' dull glitter in a rural township
transmuted to odd shapes of honour located in the duodenal
                    intestine:
transmuted to odd shapes of honour located in the duodenal intestine:
the guts of a man hung up wet and heavy,
drying on the snake fences,
swaying ghostlike from powerlines)–
Oh creditors are importinate lovers here
in the cancelled sunlight in the winter of my indebtedness,
in the grey and quiet country where wooers yell imprecations
under a faithless moon–

And in the city, between the neon blinkings, under the blanket
                    of noise,
still in the darkness lover to lover pleasantly insists
(with the same flattery ascribes to the wished-for thing all value)
that bodies open portals to each according to reciprocal
                    agreements,
and unversed hands rehearse the earth music together,
that smooth beautiful faces contrive to contort and create the
                    frog-foetus which
leaping onto the grey sheets shrieks and pries apart the lovers–

This on demand, by prior agreement in parked automobiles,
                    four dimensional doorways,
whispered moonlight rapprochements, negotiations on
                    streetcorners,
that the debt
            that the beautiful debt
                        be paid
willingly or unwillingly and with or without pleasure–

Who's that come knocking at my door?

AT ROBLIN LAKE

Did anyone plan this,
set up the co-ordinates
of experiment to bring about
an ecology of near and distant
batrachian nightingales?
—Each with a frog in his throat,
rehearsing the old springtime pap
about the glories of copulation.
If not I'd be obliged if
the accident would unhappen.

The pike and bass are admirably silent
about such things, and keep their
erotic moments *a mensa et thoro*
in cold water. After which I suppose
comes the non-judicial separation.
Which makes them somewhat misogynists?
In any case frogs are ignorant
about the delusion and snare women
represent—they brag and boast
epicene, while piscene culture doesn't.

This tangential backyard universe
I inhabit with sidereal aplomb,
tho troubled with midnight debate
by frog theologians, bogged
down in dialectics and original
sin of discursiveness
(the god of boredom at one remove,
discreetly subsidized on wooden plates)—
Next morning I make a shore-capture,
one frog like an emerald breathing,
hold the chill musical anti-body
a moment with breath held,
thinking of spores, spermatozoa, seed,
housed in this cold progenitor,
transmitting to some future species
what the wall said to Belshazzar.
And, wondering at myself, feeling
in this little green god of the flesh
the same moment of elation
I have when mind joins the body
in one great leap beyond the universe:
and stars shine thru his polka dots
as he escapes back to the lake,
and death no doubt from other monsters.

POEM

You are ill and so I lead you away
and put you to bed in the dark room
—you lie breathing softly and I hold your hand
feeling the fingertips relax as sleep comes

You will not sleep more than a few hours
and the illness is less serious than my anger or cruelty
and the dark bedroom is like a foretaste of other darknesses
to come later which all of us must endure alone
but here I am permitted to be with you

After a while in sleep your fingers clutch tightly
and I know that whatever may be happening
the fear coiled in dreams or the bright trespass of pain
there is nothing at all I can do except hold your hand
and not go away

WILDERNESS GOTHIC

Across Roblin Lake, two shores away,
they are sheathing the church spire
with new metal. Someone hangs in the sky
over there from a piece of rope,
hammering and fitting God's belly-scratcher,
working his way up along the spire
until there's nothing left to nail on—
Perhaps the workman's faith reaches beyond:
touches intangibles, wrestles with Jacob,
replacing rotten timber with pine thews,
pounds hard in the blue cave of the sky,
contends heroically with difficult problems
of gravity, sky navigation and mythopeia,
his volunteer time and labour donated to God,
minus sick benefits of course on a non-union job—

Fields around are yellowing into harvest,
nestling and fingerling are sky and water borne,
death is yodelling quiet in green woodlots,
and bodies of three young birds have disappeared
in the sub-surface of the new county highway—

That picture is incomplete, part left out
that might alter the whole Durer landscape:
gothic ancestors peer from medieval sky,
dour faces trapped in photograph albums escaping
to clop down iron roads with matched greys:
work-sodden wives groping inside their flesh
for what keeps moving and changing and flashing
beyond and past the long frozen Victorian day.
A sign of fire and brimstone? A two-headed calf
born in the barn last night? A sharp female agony?
An age and a faith moving into transition,
the dinner cold and new-baked bread a failure,
deep woods shiver and water drops hang pendant,
double yolked eggs and the house creaks a little—
Something is about to happen. Leaves are still.
Two shores away, a man hammering in the sky.
Perhaps he will fall.

POEM FOR ONE OF THE ANNETTES

Which one of you?–oh now
I recognize that tear-strained pro-
Semitic nose shaped wonderfully for
your man Murray's kisses but
he left didn't he?
       Oh Annette
                cry like hell
for Columbus Ohio and Taos New Mexico
where he is and you're not
                      As if
the world had ended and
           it has–

Or the Anita with undressed hips that
could break a man in half in bed and
big unpainted Rubens breasts affixed to
                a living woman
swinging high over Montreal
                   As if
the whole damn town was a whorehouse full
of literarily inclined millionaires with a yen
for your kind of dirty-story-book-love and
           it is–

Or Janine from Poland who's
a citizen of Canada knocked up
in Montreal by a Yank from
Columbus Ohio and
              abandoned and
the abortion took place in the Town of
Mount Royal and the foetus had
           no name–

Cry for your own bad judgment in
   loving him with good tears that
      will not
                  fall
                  but stay
in the blue beginning of every evening when
factory watchmen are coming on duty and
silent lovers are visible as moths hovering on
streetcorners
            in eccentric silver orbit
as permanent as any in
            Maisonneuve's cynical metropolis—

Cry the common sickness with ordinary tears
                              As if
they would flood the whole quasi-romantic town of
Montreal with the light of your darkness and
follow the gutters and sewers glowing down
thru sewage disposal plants by the river and
into the industrial waste of your dreams to
            the sea
            the shapeless mothering one-celled sea—

      Oh Anita, they do.

LOVE SONG

I imagine you a bitch as bad and spiteful
As Jezebel–then confuse you with Judith's tears
Shining taller than Holofernes' glinting spears...
(When you sniff the acoustics of your nose are delightful.)

Five minutes ago I was young, five minutes ago
I loved a woman...But I grew old suddenly,
Immersed in literature and decadent philosophy...
(But I can be two men if I have to.)

I will seem to you like a man seen on the street
Several times, who unaccountably disappeared,
But was not missed or ever really here...
(Unlike the man delivering beer from Porlock's Grocery.)

Coleridge knew you and maybe Shelley,
Rodomontade and hyperbole,
Rhetoric, metaphor and embroidery...
(Love is ambivalence and sex is a bully.)

Love is ambivalence and sex is a bully,
But I can be two men if I have to,
Unlike the man delivering beer from Porlock's Grocery...
(When you sniff the acoustics of your nose are delightful.)

NECROPSY OF LOVE

If it came about you died
it might be said I loved you:
love is an absolute as death is,
and neither bears false witness to the other—
But you remain alive.

No, I do not love you
                    hate the word,
that private tyranny inside a public sound,
your freedom's yours and not my own:
but hold my separate madness like a sword,
and plunge it in your body all night long.

If death shall strip our bones of all but bones,
then here's the flesh, and flesh that's drunken-sweet
as wine cups in deceptive lunar light:
reach up your hand and turn the moonlight off,
and maybe it was never there at all,
so never promise anything to me:
but reach across the darkness with your hand,
reach across the distance of tonight,
and touch the moving moment once again
                    before you fall asleep—

THE WINEMAKER'S BEAT-ÉTUDE

I am picking wild grapes last year
in a field
            dragging down great lianas of vine
tearing at 20 feet of heavy infinite purple
having a veritable tug-o-war with Bacchus
who grins at me delightedly in the high branches
of one of those stepchild appletrees
unloved by anything but tent caterpillars
and ghosts of old settlers
become such strangers here
I am thinking what the grapes are thinking
become part of their purple mentality
that is
            I am satisfied with the sun and
eventual fermenting bubble-talk together
then transformed and glinting with coloured lights in
            a GREAT JEROBOAM
that booms inside from the land beyond the world
In fact
I am satisfied with my own shortcomings letting
myself happen then
                        I'm surrounded by Cows
black and white ones with tails
At first I'm uncertain how to advise them
in mild protest or frank manly invective
then realize that the cows are right
it's me that's the trespasser
                        Of course they are curious
perhaps wish to see me perform
                        I moo off key
                        I bark like a man
                        laugh like a dog
                        and talk like God
                        hoping

they'll go away so Bacchus and I can get on with it
Then I get logical thinking if there was ever a
feminine principle cows are it and why not but
what would so many females want?
I address them like Brigham Young hastily
"No, that's out! I won't do it!
                    Absolutely not!"
Contentment steals back among all this femininity
thinking cows are together so much they must be nearly
all lesbians fondling each other's dugs by moonlight why
Sappho's own star-reaching soul shines inward and outward
from the soft Aegean islands in these eyes and
I am dissolved like a salt lick instantly oh
                    Sodium chloride!
                    Prophylactic acid!
                    Gamma particles (in suspension)!
                    After shave lotion!
                    Rubbing alcohol!
                              suddenly
I become the whole damn feminine principle so
happily noticing little tendrils of affection steal
out from each to each unshy honest encompassing
golden calves in Israel and slum babies in Canada and
a millionaire's brat left squalling on the toilet seat in
Rockefeller Center
                    O my sisters
                    I give purple milk!

NEWS REPORTS AT AMELIASBURG

In the night of my sleep at embassies
in Hong Kong and Cairo and humid oil capitals
of Arab republics in New York and Moscow
in London and Paris in Accra and Rome
the people say no
philosophers search for new absolutes
hopheads pry into their negative psyche
Bedouins march thru stoplights of sand dunes
pickets circle round factories with banners
negro non-violence reaches invisible barriers
at houses abandoned by wealthy distillers
rocks break the glass and death discolours the gutters
battalions of students are shouting their slogans
and the centuries roll onward like mass-produced coffins
to carry the world wherever the world may be going

        At Delphi the Oracle gives odds on war and Leonidas
turns aside from the pass at Thermopylae
to attack the Americans
Hannibal drives his elephants into Toronto
Cleopatra and Antony have signed a treaty with Caesar
to burn down Chicago and destroy Los Angeles studios
Alexander turns from the gates of the Ganges
and moves with his generals and phalanx to bulldoze the Kremlin
while the eunuch priests conspire in Assyria
to defoliate the Vietnamese rice fields of bananas
At night in our own bodies comes a small dark whisper
relayed here from the beginning of human time
where ancient hunters confer with stones and tree-spirits
their campfires throwing enormous shadows on the forest
and witch-doctors dance in our blood forever

Only behind the centuries is something near silence
before the glaciers turned into ice cubes
before there was man
no young students to ponder old questions
of right and wrong and be sure that life is no bargain
but more important than sleep is
tho windows are breaking around me

The groundhog pushes a stone to the mouth of his burrow
the goldfinch repairs his nest with a patchwork of sunset
the fox removes his teeth to a glass for safekeeping
squirrels retire to a rotten tree and the damn thing blossoms
pike in the monocle eye of the lake have switched off the planets
I have unbuckled my sword and lay there beside them
the sun has gone down in my village

DEATH OF JOHN F. KENNEDY

On first hearing of his death
no one believed it
           not for a moment
               for three years
television and newspapers
had made him a god of our time
and gods are indestructable
           But he was only a man
and the man's body is gone now
leaving behind the uninhabited legend
of himself which is a little like
an empty suit of armour made
by a Bronx tailor for maybe
Richard Coeur de Lion
at a costume party
for idiots

He (Kennedy) was one of the famous
for whom poems get written like
Dylan Thomas–Roosevelt–Nicolai Lenin
(only after their dying lifetime of course)
And of those three only Thomas had the
endearing fictional qualities of being
real most of the time 24 hours later than
the second-hand reported outrageous events
of his life and
           I mourn for Caitlin who
in jigtime undeniably becomes
minor fiction and has a ghostlike sound

And come to think of it
                    I mourn Lee Oswald
                    as well as Kennedy who
was a normal sort of do-gooder god whereas
Oswald is prototype of the deranged assassin
                    he murdered Caesar and Lincoln
                    Archduke Ferdinand and all those titles
                    sparkling in the dust
                    attempted King Mithridates many times
                    but "he died old"
and just the other day downtown
made a pass at me in a poolroom
                    Yes
                    I mourn Lee Oswald
because he was a kind of Typhoid Mary
who had the disease in its pure form
one disease we all have
                    ANIMAL HATE
that seems so handcuffed to human vitality
linked and lobotomized to the best things
If Oswald had lived
perhaps we could have isolated it
in a test tube
                    labelled "Oswald Extract"
or "Very Dangerous" and "Much Too Human"
part of the obscure pride and shame
of being homo sapiens that might be used
to cross cerebral galaxies

                    (Is that why I mourn Lee Oswald?
because he was much too human?
and as a result was never alive really?
Typhoid Mary with a high-powered mailorder rifle
infecting future colonies across the nebulae
with hate
                    but just a minute
                    Hey now
                    if only I'd killed Oswald
in the poolroom downtown when I had my chance
                    See what I mean?)

And thinking
how the mind empties of passion and speculation
how the population of earth is replaced
every hundred years the Caesars and street cleaners
and fathers and mothers and painfully awkward
adolescents with pimples without furore and
no one escapes in the outcry only
pyramids and some broken bits of pottery
survive the long howl of a funeral oration
                        and out in the suburbs all the time
a mother of six
                        is quietly having another baby

                        And I mourn Kennedy
                        the man everybody knows
—strangers who never met
connected by a dead man's compass points
and vectors penetrating now
                        like battery terminals:
for which the power supply
jams under a heavy load of messages from
huntsmen falling asleep standing in snowstorms
in the 2nd Ice Age forever and Sumerian shepherd
kings catching cold and soon dead of the sniffles and
messages from rock cairns in Transylvania
and exiles in a Roman province from Hyannisport
and Sierra Maestra and Crimea and silence:
for which the power supply
in an inflection of a subordinate clause
                        on television
                        a remembered grin

ON THE DECIPHERMENT OF "LINEAR B"
(By Michael Ventris and associates)

Grammatic structure first, then phonetic values:
Ventris mailing progress reports to philologists
for comment (by air across the Atlantic):
the endgame–all the dusty Cretan sibilants
hissing delightedly back to life on scholar tongues,
whispering possible gossip to the co-translators
–that turned out to be inventories,
amphorae in warehouses, wine long vanished,
dried to red dust in the guts of Mycenaean warriors;
listings of clergy reserves, military property:
"Horse vehicle, painted red, supplied with reins";
words, preserved like nothing machines make,
perfect, unflawed, the same.

We see them (dramatic as hell), the code-breakers,
in shirt sleeves, drinking gallons of coffee:
gowned Oxford dons, real estate brokers,
American academics–a linguistic orgy,
broken by twitterings of girlish excitement,
punctuated with cries of discovery.

It turns out Minos was maybe an expatriate
Greek, who said to hell with hiero-
glyphic symbols: brought in the smith Daedalus
(a bad mistake re Pasiphae's morals)
to promote Greek investment, Linear B and stud poker–
Well anyway, Ventris figured it out,
and anyone can sit down after work reading
comic books or Agamemnon's diaries now.

But Knossos did burn, its flaming windows
signalled the stars 3,000 years ago:
when men died foetal, rolled into blackened balls,
and women, abandoned by children and lovers,
fled to the palace upper rooms with skirts on fire:
and over the island a south wind blowing–

HOCKEY PLAYERS

What they worry about most is injuries
                broken arms and legs and
fractured skulls opening so doctors
can see such bloody beautiful things almost
not quite happening in the bone rooms
                as they happen outside
And the referee?
                He's right there on the ice
not out of sight among the roaring blue gods
of a game played for passionate stockbrokers
children wearing business suits
and a nation of television agnostics
who never agree with the referee and applaud
when he falls flat on his face

                On a breakaway
the centreman carrying the puck
his wings trailing a little
                on both sides why
I've seen the aching glory of a resurrection
                in their eyes
                if they score
but crucifixion's agony to lose
—the game?

                We sit up there in the blues
bored and sleepy and suddenly three men

break down the ice in roaring feverish speed and
we stand up in our seats with such a rapid pouring
of delight exploding out of self to join them why
theirs and our orgasm is the rocket stipend
for skating thru the smoky end boards out
of sight and climbing up the appalachian highlands
and racing breast to breast across laurentian barrens
over hudson's diamond bay and down the treeless tundra where
auroras are tubercular and awesome and
stopping isn't feasible or possible or lawful
but we have to and we have to
                              laugh because we must and
stop to look at self and one another but
            our opponent's never geography
                              or distance why
            it's men
            –just men?

And how do the players feel about it
this combination of ballet and murder?
For years a Canadian specific
to salve the anguish of inferiority
by being good at something the Americans aren't
And what's the essence of a game like this
which takes a ten year fragment of a man's life
replaced with love that lodges in his brain
            and substitutes for reason?
Besides the fear of injuries
is it the difficulty of ever really overtaking
a hard black rubber disc?
–Boys playing a boy's game in a permanent childhood
with a screaming coach who insists on winning
sports-writer-critics and the crowd gone mad?
–And the worrying wives wanting you to quit and
your aching body stretched on the rubbing table
thinking of money in owners' pockets that might be yours
the butt-slapping camaraderie and the self indulgence
of allowing yourself to be a hero and knowing
everything ends in a pot-belly

Out on the ice can all these things be forgotten
in swift and skilled delight of speed?
—roaring out the endboards out the city
streets and high up where laconic winds
whisper litanies for a fevered hockey player
Or racing breast to breast and never stopping
over rooftops of the world and all together
sing the song of winning all together
sing the song of money all together

        (and out in the suburbs
there's the six-year-old kid
whose reflexes were all wrong
who always fell down and hurt himself and cried
and never learned to skate
        with his friends)

JOINT ACCOUNT

The myth includes Canada,
inside the brain's small country:
my backyard is the Rocky Mountain trench
–wading all summer in glacier meltwater,
hunters with flint axes stumble south–
I take deed and title to ancient badlands
of Alberta around Red Deer:
and dinosaurs peer into Calgary office buildings–
Dead Beothucks of Newfoundland track down my blood;
Dorsets on the whale-coloured Beaufort Sea
carve my brain into small ivory fossils
that show what it was like to be alive
before the skin tents blew down–

The slope of mountain breast and the wind's words,
the moon's white breathing–these are hers:
her eyes' black flashing are the continent's anger
  my letters fall to silence at her land's white foot,
and waves have washed away her answer
In the long body of the land I saw your own,
the mountain peaks,
the night of stars,
the words I did not speak,
and you did not,
that yet were spoken–

But reality is an overdrawn bank account,
my myths and cheques both bounce,
the creditors close in;
and all the dead men,
chanting hymns,
tunnel towards me underground.

EVERGREEN CEMETERY

I guess it is ever green...
and what's sure if green isn't?
Me standing here in death's
ceded town
            in full summer
the dead down there unfreezing comfortably
the cold miserable rain untouching them
outnumbering all to hell the last newcomers:
1 human, 2 chipmunks, some squirrels–
Child me (subtract 30 years)
yelling down the rotting mausoleum vent:
            "Hoo-hoo–wake up!"
The dead inside silent
               silent now.

So–the swaggerers flaunt
over graves an appropriate green panache,
the braggarts delve into dumb roots,
and the lovers join an unemotional passion,
as earth shapes and reshapes itself
              again and again.

But the dead are wholehearted about being dead,
no half measures no shilly-shallying:
they're committed, dedicated
              to purposelessness.
And I get a grim glee from all the high-sounding
old aspirations and clichés ending in damp ground,
glee close to grief maybe, a hangman's gladness:
if that's being human it's best done with.

But it's too complicated to sum up
in telling phrase or easy pessimism,
syllogism or denouement...
I've seen this same graveyard sunlight
at a beach mottled on a girl's flesh,
and groped for it under a blanket:
I've seen these trees spilling down mountains
that I trudged up sweating,
and loved for their banners' brightness.

Well
    I've no business in this damn place,
not yet anyway with the taverns open,
tho my mother has:
inept christian that she was,
bumbling among the granite colossi
searching for her redeemer...
But I remember her savage grey face
before she died in a drugged fever,
and nurse telling me she'd stuffed her false teeth
up her rectum (in a pleased shocked voice):
        that sharpened elemental
        grinning face
        with empty jaws which
        almost as I watched bit
                hard on death.

Which reminds me I'd better hurry and get out
of here before the gates close.

AT THE QUINTE HOTEL

I am drinking
I am drinking beer with yellow flowers
in underground sunlight
and you can see that I am a sensitive man
And I notice that the bartender is a sensitive man too
so I tell him about his beer
I tell him the beer he draws
is half fart and half horse piss
and all wonderful yellow flowers
But the bartender is not quite
so sensitive as I supposed he was
the way he looks at me now
and does not appreciate my exquisite analogy
Over in one corner two guys
are quietly making love
in the brief prelude to infinity
Opposite them a peculiar fight
enables the drinkers to lay aside
their comic books and watch with interest
as I watch with interest
A wiry little man slugs another guy
then tracks him bleeding into the toilet
and slugs him to the floor again
with ugly red flowers on the tile
three minutes later he roosters over
to the table where his drunk friend sits
with another friend and slugs both
of em ass-over-electric-kettle
so I have to walk around
on my way for a piss
Now I am a sensitive man
so I say to him mildly as hell
"You shouldn'ta knocked over that good beer
with them beautiful flowers in it"

So he says to me "Come on"
so I Come On
like a rabbit with weak kidneys I guess
like a yellow streak charging
on flower power I suppose
& knock the shit outa him & sit on him
(he is just a little guy)
and say reprovingly
"Violence will get you nowhere this time chum
  Now you take me
  I am a sensitive man
  and would you believe I write poems?"
  But I could see the doubt in his upside down face
  in fact in all the faces
"What kinda poems?"
"Flower poems"
"So tell us a poem"
  I got off the little guy but reluctantly
  for he was comfortable
  and told them this poem
  They crowded around me with tears
  in their eyes and wrung my hands feelingly
  for my pockets for
  it was a heart-warming moment for Literature
  and moved by the demonstrable effect
  of great Art and the brotherhood of people I remarked
"–the poem oughta be worth some beer"
  It was a mistake of terminology
  for silence came
  and it was brought home to me in the tavern
  that poems will not really buy beer or flowers
  or a goddam thing
  and I was sad
  for I am a sensitive man

WATCHING TRAINS

Indian boys at Nakina and Sioux Lookout
from tent towns in the bush
and blueberry shacks by a railway siding
($1.50 a basket in bargain summer)
with schoolmarm passenger distributing
replicas of the new Canadian flag
Boys with their mouths open
some missing part supplied by trains
Thought will not come to them nor speech
they have no words for department stores
or pictographs for elevators going fifty
miles an hour into the sky
They watch the train
dumbfound as newfallen snow
            blank eyes and blank minds
that do not follow down the whispering rails
or think of anything
until the train goes
and birds dispute the ownership of silence

Hours or miles
later in the snowbush
with summer gone
they hear a diesel hoot
like blood that shrieks inside their toenails
trains
inside their inward eye
from all directions bearing down on them
from deadfalls under scrub cedar
and burned pine skeletons
and traplines where the red-eyed weasel
snarls in a wire noose
and foxes gnaw their forelegs
free from steel

the trains
converge from snowhung poplar coverts
mooseyards and small creeks
their bubble music choked with ice
the diesels vector in
And rails run down the day's horizon
a white eye slants on hogback hills
thru midnight zero pullmans pass
and spike their echoes to the trees . . . .

Trains
        things
                thought itself
no capital letters tattooed presto
on people
like Mr. Tecumseh and Mr. Hiawatha
or Joe Something
faces are faces
The skulls contain
pictures of things
woodsmoke messages
the melted circle of snow
around living trees
old loved rifles
the price of blueberries
people
happening memories
maybe death
and trains
trains
And will see them like small glory
among snarling dogs and chewed bones in the snow
as wind invades the tarpaper mansions
till June and the bush raspberries come . . . .

COMPLAINT LODGED WITH L.C.B.O.
BY A CITIZEN OF UPPER RUMBELOW

I am driving thru town with a case
of beer in the back seat
with two empties in it
which is illegal see and
I notice this cop in the rear
vision mirror following me on
a motorcycle and for
a minute I feel peculiar
At the stop street I carefully
STOP
          and the cop stops too not
to be caught that easy
and I see him watching how
I sit so I sit up straight as
'The Motorist' by Praxiteles
excavated by Henry Ford 4
from under a million traffic tickets
of dead Greeks speeding in Argos agora
or was it 'Hermes' or 'Pallas Athene'
and not 'The Motorist' at all?
                              Anyway
there's that cop on my tail
and I signal a left turn
and he signals a left turn
I signal a right turn
and he signals a right turn
and I think what the hell
is this a game or something and
maybe didn't I brush my teeth
this morning and grin with all of them
in the rear view mirror and figure
out a hand signal for a ground loop
and inverted Immelmann plus
an unorthodox Christiana I learned
once on Parnassus which lofts
me among the treetops there encountering
God (hi pops) 50 feet above the
business section we stop to talk and
I ask him about that damned cop
of his and (ha-ha) how I fooled him

But he's parked waiting
for me at the Presbyterian
steeple that got struck by lightning
like a blue cop-angel who's
a dead ringer for the prophet Isaiah
And I says "You didn't make the turn signal"
and he says "It ain't in the book"
and I guess that's so it ain't so
I get fined fifteen bucks
and let off with a warning
but just the same—

FROM THE CHIN P'ING MEI

Fifty men at arms with bows and lances
from the River Prefect. From the District Yamen
twenty more. Two hundred from General Chang.
The booms of drums, the clang of gongs—
She would have been frightened, my little one,
if she were alive and her palanquin,
passing through the South Gate at noonday,
had encountered the funeral procession
of a dead lady—she would have wept.

BOUNDARIES

In all these southern counties
                with English names
York   Dufferin   Hastings   Northumberland
              stood the great trees
     gone for a hundred years now
and the mannered expressionless urban names
              mark the boundaries
insert themselves like worn silver shillings
     in mouths of city people
     to spend on tiny vistas
             in parking lots
                 fenced backyards

Far north the still rich vulgarity
              to match
a man-breaking country
    "The Torngat Mountains"
             east of nowhere
westerly
    "Telegraph Creek"
        "100 Mile House"
northerly
        "Arctic Red River"
          "Tuktoyatuk"
Nobody speaks those names without feeling
the tongue touch rank bear-steak
or prickling devil's club
and remembers mountain land
             the iron north
beyond the last streetlight
drowned in snow
teeth chatter over mere pronunciation
biting the stammered name
to pieces held there a moment
in a man's cold mouth
the edge of our loneliness

WHOEVER YOU ARE

If birds look in the window odd beings
look back and birds must stay birds.
If dogs gaze upward at yellow oblongs
of warmth, bark for admittance
to hot caves high above the street
among the things with queer fur,
the dogs are turned to dogs, and longing
wags its tail and turns invisible.

Clouds must be clouds always, even if
they've not decided what to be at all,
and trees trees, stones stones, unnoticed,
the magic power of anything is gone.   ·
But sometimes when the moonlight disappears,
with you in bed and nodding half awake,
I have not known exactly who you were,
and choked and could not speak your name....

FURTHER DEPONENT SAITH NOT

I am trapped in an old house
full of paint brushes and hammers
saws and spirit levels and things
which I am supposed to use
for some constructive purpose
but I drink a drink of rye instead
and test the canned fruit for fermentation
in the cellar
whose rafters I am supposed to jack up
with a house jack
                and indeed do jack up
with a house jack
And God goes whooping thru the timbers
and shakes hands with all the door knobs
mistaking them for businessmen
and U.S. Steel closes at 1984
but I prefer Seagram's 83
which stays open all the time
And there are 16 King James Bibles
and 12 hymn books in that cellar
without a word of a lie
and moved by some tender religious impulse
I sing 'Throw Out the Lifeline'
to the dead who once lived
in this 100-year-old house
and were all music lovers
And somebody knocks at the door
and I figure it must be a bill collector
and I figure there must be a town out there
for there to be bill collectors
in any event he's unwelcome
In any case I have the Seagram's
and saws and hammers and paint brushes
and climb the walls to an attic
and sing from the roof at God
having belched loudly to secure his attention
sing 'Show Me the Way to Go Home'
but he ignores the melodious sounds

And nails get bent and glass painted
and dead feelings hurt and it's a long time
till death a long way since birth in this house
I once lived in where I sit writing and drinking
rye and the ghosts of all the Purdys who ever lived
make hissing sounds out loud and cuss me good
But it's no use
I absolutely refuse to contribute to Foreign Missionaries
I got the Seagram's
and it seems like I've never been
anywhere else but here
So I hammer a nail vindictively
it bends
I clean a window energetically
it breaks
and I cut my finger on the damn glass
Anyway I got the Seagram's
       —no by god I haven't
            someone drank it the bastard
The fridge motor buzzes and drones
silence grimaces to itself
the walls creak and mutter like imbeciles
and there is someone at the door

THERE IS SOMEONE AT THE DOOR

who wishes to deliver my death certificate
and a pleasing floral tribute for shut-ins
title deed in fee simple for one used lawn mower
absolution for your sins absolutely

      Bring out your dead and come yourself
           I am not at home
               I am not at home

ROBLIN'S MILLS (2)

The wheels stopped
and the murmur of voices
behind the flume's tremble
stopped
      and the wind-high ships
that sailed from Rednersville
to the sunrise ports of Europe
are delayed somewhere
in a toddling breeze
The black millpond
turns an unreflecting eye
to look inward
like an idiot child
locked in the basement
when strangers come
whizzing past on the highway
above the dark green valley
a hundred yards below
The mill space is empty
even stones are gone
where hands were shaken
and walls enclosed laughter
saved up and brought here
from the hot fields
where all stories
are rolled into one
And white dust floating
above the watery mumble
and bright human sounds
to shimmer among the pollen
where bees dance now
Of all these things
no outline remains
no shadow on the soft air
no bent place in the heat glimmer
where the heavy walls pressed

And some of those who vanished
lost children of the time
kept after school
left alone in a graveyard
who may not change
or ever grow six inches
in one hot summer
or turn where the great herons
graze the sky's low silver
—stand between the hours
in a rotting village
near the weed-grown eye
that looks into itself
deep in the black crystal
that holds and contains
the substance of shadows
manner and custom
          of the inarticulate
departures and morning rumours
gestures and almost touchings
announcements and arrivals
gossip of someone's marriage
when a girl or tired farm woman
whose body suddenly blushes
beneath a faded house dress
with white expressionless face
turns to her awkward husband
to remind him of something else
The black millpond
                    holds them
movings and reachings and fragments
the gear and tackle of living
under the water eye
all things laid aside
                    discarded
                         forgotten
but they had their being once
and left a place to stand on

THE COUNTRY NORTH OF BELLEVILLE

Bush land scrub land—
      Cashel Township and Wollaston
Elzevir McClure and Dungannon
green lands of Weslemkoon Lake
where a man might have some
      opinion of what beauty
is and none deny him
             for miles—

Yet this is the country of defeat
where Sisyphus rolls a big stone
year after year up the ancient hills
picnicking glaciers have left strewn
with centuries' rubble
             backbreaking days
             in the sun and rain
when realization seeps slow in the mind
without grandeur or self deception in
             noble struggle
of being a fool—

A country of quiescence and still distance
a lean land
      not like the fat south
with inches of black soil on
      earth's round belly—
And where the farms are
      it's as if a man stuck
both thumbs in the stony earth and pulled

      it apart
      to make room
enough between the trees
for a wife
      and maybe some cows and
      room for some
of the more easily kept illusions—
And where the farms have gone back
to forest
      are only soft outlines
      shadowy differences—

Old fences drift vaguely among the trees
            a pile of moss-covered stones
gathered for some ghost purpose
has lost meaning under the meaningless sky
            —they are like cities under water
and the undulating green waves of time
            are laid on them—

This is the country of our defeat
            and yet
during the fall plowing a man
might stop and stand in a brown valley of the furrows
            and shade his eyes to watch for the same
            red patch mixed with gold
            that appears on the same
            spot in the hills
            year after year
            and grow old
plowing and plowing a ten-acre field until
the convolutions run parallel with his own brain

And this is a country where the young
            leave quickly
unwilling to know what their fathers know
or think the words their mothers do not say—

Herschel Monteagle and Faraday
lakeland rockland and hill country
a little adjacent to where the world is
a little north of where the cities are and
sometime
we may go back there
            to the country of our defeat
Wollaston Elzevir and Dungannon
and Weslemkoon lake land
where the high townships of Cashel
            McClure and Marmora once were—
But it's been a long time since
and we must enquire the way
            of strangers—

MY '48 PONTIAC

All winter long it wouldn't start
standing in the yard covered with snow
I'd go out at 10 below zero and coax
and say
        "Where's your pride?"
and kick it disgustedly
Finally snow covered everything
but television aerials and the world was
a place nobody came to
so white it couldn't be looked at
before nothing was something
But the old Pontiac lay there
affirming its identity
like some prehistoric vegetarian
stupidly unaware of snow
waiting for Tyrannosaurus Rex
to come along and bite off its fenders
"You no good American Pontiac you
(I'd say)
you're a disgrace to General Motors"
then go out and hitch up the dog team
When June hurried by it still wouldn't start
only stop
and the wreckers hauled it away

Now and then I go to visit my old friend
at Bud's Auto Wreckers
being sentimental about rubber and metal
I think it's glad to see me
and wags both tail lights
a true heart thumping eagerly
under the torn seat covers
I sit behind the wheel
on a parched August afternoon
and we drive thru a glitter of broken glass
among suicides and automotive murders
mangled chryslers and volkswagens
metal twisted into a look
of fierce helplessness
reversed violence in hunchback shapes
and containing it still
waiting to explode outward

We drive between dismantled buicks and
studebakers and one stuckup old cadillac
driven to Bud's by a doddering chauffeur
who used to play poker with Roman chariot drivers
and a silent crumpled grey plymouth
with bloodstains on the instrument panel
where a girl died
a '41 de soto with all the chrome gone
still excited from drag races
and quivering blondes whose bottoms it liked
My last visit was by moonlight and flashlight
to Bud's Auto Wreckers
where the old Pontiac waited
I turned the speedometer back to 5000 miles
changed the oil
polished the headlights to look at death
adjusted the rear view mirror to look at life
gave it back its ownership card
and went away
puzzled by things

TRANSIENT

Riding the boxcars out of Winnipeg in a
morning after rain so close to
the violent sway of fields it's
like running and running
naked with summer in your mouth and
the guy behind you grunts and says
"Got a smoke?"

Being a boy scarcely a moment and you
hear the rumbling iron roadbed singing
under the wheels at night and a door jerking open
mile after dusty mile riding into Regina with
the dust storm crowding behind you and
a guy you hardly even spoke to
nudges your shoulder chummily and says
"Got a smoke?"

Riding into the Crow's Nest mountains with
your first beard itching and a
hundred hungry guys fanning out thru
the shabby whistlestops for handouts and
not even a sandwich for two hundred miles
only the high mountains and knowing
what it's like to be not quite a child
any more and listening to the tough men
talk of women and talk of the way things are
in 1937

Riding down in the spit-grey sea level morning
thru dockyard streets and dingy dowager houses
with ocean a jump away and the sky beneath you
in puddles on Water Street and an old Indian woman
pushing her yawning scratching daughter
onto a balcony to yell at the boy-man passing
"Want some fun?–come on up" and the girl just
come from riding the shrieking bedspring bronco
all the up and down night to a hitchpost morning
full of mothers and dirt and lice and
        hardly the place for a princess
        of the Coast Salish
                (My dove my little one
tonight there will be wine and the loins of a dozen men
to pin you down in the outlying lands of sleep
innocent as a child
        awaiting the last of all your bridegrooms)

Stand in the swaying boxcar doorway
moving cast away from the sunset and
after a while the eyes digest a country and
the belly perceives a mapmaker's vision
in dust and dirt on the face and hands here
its smell drawn deep thru the nostrils down
to the lungs and spurts thru blood stream
campaigns in the lower intestine
        and chants love songs to the kidneys
After a while there is no arrival and
no departure possible any more
you are where you were always going
and the shape of home is under your fingernails
the borders of yourself grown into certainty
the identity of forests that were always nameless
the selfhood of rivers that are changing always
the nationality of riding freight trains thru the depression
over long green plains and high mountain country
with the best and worst of a love that's not to be spoken
and a guy right behind you says then
"Got a smoke?"
You give him one and stand in the boxcar doorway
or looking out the window of a Montreal apartment
or running the machines in a Vancouver factory
–you stand there growing older

Index of titles

ABOUT BEING A MEMBER OF OUR ARMED FORCES/58
ARCTIC RHODODENDRONS/59
AT ROBLIN LAKE/84
AT THE MOVIES/73
AT THE QUINTE HOTEL/106

BOUNDARIES/112

CARIBOO HORSES, THE/24
COLLECTING THE SQUARE ROOT OF MINUS ONE/82
COMPLAINT LODGED WITH THE L.C.B.O./110
COUNTRY NORTH OF BELLEVILLE, THE/118
COUNTRY OF THE YOUNG, THE/77

DARK LANDSCAPE/36
DEATH OF JOHN F. KENNEDY/96
DREAM OF HAVANA/54
DRUNK TANK, THE/26
DYLAN/49

EVERGREEN CEMETERY/104

FIDEL CASTRO IN REVOLUTIONARY SQUARE/50
FROM THE CHIN P'ING MEI/111
FURTHER DEPONENT SAITH NOT/114

HELPING MY WIFE GET SUPPER/79
HOCKEY PLAYERS/100
HOMBRE/52
HOME-MADE BEER/48
HOUSE GUEST/80

IDIOT'S SONG/39
INTERRUPTION/38

JOINT ACCOUNT/103

LAMENT FOR THE DORSETS/71
LATE RISING AT ROBLIN LAKE/25
LOVE SONG/90

MARRIED MAN'S SONG/42
MY '48 PONTIAC/120
MY GRANDFATHER'S COUNTRY/40
MY GRANDFATHER TALKING–30 YEARS AGO/28

NECROPSY OF LOVE/91
NEWS REPORTS AT AMELIASBURG/94
NOTES ON A FICTIONAL CHARACTER/46

OLD ALEX/29
ONE RURAL WINTER/32
ON THE DECIPHERMENT OF "LINEAR B"/99
OVER THE HILLS IN THE RAIN, MY DEAR/19

PERCY LAWSON/44
POEM/86
POEM FOR ONE OF THE ANNETTES/88

ROAD TO NEWFOUNDLAND, THE/17
ROBLIN'S MILLS (1)/34
ROBLIN'S MILLS (2)/116
RUNNERS, THE/21

SCULPTORS, THE/67
SERGEANT JACKSON/56
SPRING SONG/30

TRANSIENT/122
TREES AT THE ARCTIC CIRCLE/62
TURNING POINT, THE/60

WASHDAY/64
WATCHING TRAINS/108
WHAT DO THE BIRDS THINK/75
WHEN I SAT DOWN TO PLAY THE PIANO/69
WHOEVER YOU ARE/113
WILDERNESS GOTHIC/87
WINEMAKER'S BEAT-ÉTUDE, THE/92
WINTER AT ROBLIN LAKE/34

Index of first lines

Across Roblin Lake, two shores away/87
All hours the day begins one may/25
All winter long it wouldn't start/120
A man keeps hammering at the door/26
Animal bones and some mossy tent rings/71
An oil drum full/64
Are they exiles here from the rest of the world?/75
At 100 Mile House the cowboys ride in rolling/24
A. Y. Jackson for instance/77

Brother, the wind of this place is cold/21
Bush land scrub land/118

Did anyone plan this/84

"85 years old, that miserable alcoholic/29

Fifty men at arms with bows and lances/111
For a week the flies have been terrible/36
For two months we quarrelled over socialism   poetry
    how to boil water/80

Give me peace from you/39
Going thru cases and cases/67
Grammatic structure first, then phonetic values:/99

He begins to speak/50
He cometh forth hurriedly from his tent/69
Highway 62/40

I am drinking/106
I am driving thru town with a case/110
I am picking wild grapes last year/92
I am trapped in an old house/114
If birds look in the window odd beings/113
If it came about you died/91
I guess it is ever green.../104
I imagine you a bitch as bad and spiteful/90
In all these southern counties/112
Indian boys at Nakina and Sioux Lookout/108
In the long grass lying/56

In the night of my sleep at embassies/94
I read him on the bus going/49
I was justly annoyed 10 years ago/48

–Met briefly in Havana/52
My foot has pushed a fire ahead of me/17

Not now boy not now/28

Old father me/30
On first hearing of his death/96
Over northern Canada/60

Remember the early days of the phony war/58
Riding the boxcars out of Winnipeg in a/122

Seeing the sky darken & the fields/34
Sitting with Lawson in 1954/44
Something basically satisfying real and valid/79

Talking to Red Chinese sailors/54
The mill was torn down last year/34
The myth includes Canada/103
The setting is really unreal/73
The wheels stopped/116
They are 18 inches long/62
They are small purple surprises/59
To owe money–this the creditors think important/82
Trapped/32

We are walking back from the Viking site/19
What they worry about most is injuries/100
When he makes love to the young girl/42
When the new house was built/38
Which one of you?–oh now/88
With cobwebs between elbows and knees/46

You are ill and so I lead you away/86